Activism; v. Movement/History

Homosexual Liberation

Homosexual Liberation

A Personal View

JOHN MURPHY

PRAEGER PUBLISHERS
New York • Washington • London

PRAEGER PUBLISHERS
111 Fourth Avenue, New York, N.Y. 10003, U.S.A.
5, Cromwell Place, London SW7 2JL, England

Published in the United States of America in 1971
by Praeger Publishers, Inc.

© 1971 by Praeger Publishers, Inc.

Library of Congress Catalog Card Number: 75–145950

Printed in the United States of America

contents

Homosexual Liberation

1  *families and friends*

RECENTLY THERE HAS been a spate of articles concerning homosexuality, pro and con, in leading magazines and newspapers. Much attention has been focused on homosexuals who are now able to come out after years of hiding. This book is not one of those "confessions." Rather, it is a statement of experiences from a new generation, a generation not interested in justifying ourselves so much as changing our lives. The need for this change has brought me to write this book—and to face some difficult problems along the way.

Soon after I became involved in the gay liberation movement, I decided to tell my family that I was a homosexual. There was no urgent need to do so; the decision was simply one of the results of a growing dissatisfaction that I felt at hiding an important part of myself. Although my mother and stepfather separated shortly before my stepfather's recent death, I tried to keep lines of communication open with both of them. For a variety of reasons, it was much easier to do so with my mother. She is a sensible, intelligent, good-hearted woman who encouraged me from childhood to do what I really wanted to do. When I left home at eighteen to put myself through college, she let me know that I could always count on the family, but also that I was on my own, for good. I have always been able to discuss personal matters with her, if I wished, or keep them to myself. She does not pry.

But, like most American mothers, she wants to see her children happy. She had met some of the women I knew, and she liked a few of them very much. Occasionally she would inquire about one girl or another, and I would tell her how they were. One night, however, on one of my rare visits home, I gave her a more complicated answer than she had expected. When she mentioned a girl I had known for years, I said she was fine and added that I was not involved with this girl now; in fact, I was involved with a man. My mother at first thought I was joking; she then went into another room and became extremely upset. I immediately felt guilty. I had not really thought of the consequences for her; I had only thought about expressing what was on my mind, at all costs. But, later in the evening, as we talked more calmly, a lot of things became clear.

She was still very distressed. Her admitted daydreams about a happy marriage for me, grandchildren, my carrying on the family line now seemed impossible and even ridiculous. Her first reaction was withdrawal. She didn't want to hear about it, not from me, not at that moment. She would have preferred knowing nothing rather than the truth. And I felt guilty for upsetting her. But I remembered that I had not, in fact, done *anything* wrong, either in my personal choice of homosexuality or in my decision to tell her. I believed that my homosexuality was part of a good way to live; I had told her about it because of this and because I was tired of pretending that it did not exist. And she realized that I wasn't a different person simply because I had told her more about myself. The only thing that had radically changed in the last few hours was her conception of me, not my actual self.

But she was still upset. She had been raised in the same country as I. She had read the same things about homosexuality and heard the same jokes. Homosexuality was a bad thing. To her, it was perhaps a sickness; more likely, it was a sort of perversion, something dirty that should not be spoken about. My confident declarations that homosexuality was definitely good did not reassure her.

We let the matter lie. This is the usual outcome of confrontations between homosexuals and their parents, I have found. It is supposed to be an unspoken understanding, but usually parents simply try to forget what has happened. And that is probably the best solution in most cases; it is unfair to torture your parents with a reality that is horrible for them, however pleasant it may be for you.

However, when I decided to write this book, another wave of complications arose. It was relatively easy to tell my mother I was a homosexual. It is also relatively easy to be a homosexual in New York City (my home now), where homosexuals have strength at least in numbers. It was another matter entirely to announce it to the world. I was prepared to handle any adverse reactions; in fact, I hoped there would be a great many, because the aggressive, self-defining anger that is rising in myself and other homosexuals will only be increased by the opposition of heterosexuals. But all that was on the abstract level of the possible. I also had to consider the concrete results that my declaration might have on my family.

Two of my four younger sisters are still in elementary school. They live in a small town in the South, the town where I was raised. It is a very pretty place, a bedroom suburb for a large city. There are pleasant homes with nice lawns, neighborhood cookouts, town fairs. Everyone knows everyone else and has a friendly interest in what is going on in the town. But, when I grew up there, I always felt vaguely discontented, and, at times, I was frustrated almost beyond endurance. There were feelings that I had, emotions that I could not understand, which made me feel that I was different from most of the boys I was growing up with. In that kind of situation, different means worse. A child or adolescent knows better than to assert his individuality before he is strong enough to endure the reaction he will provoke. I studied hard, harder than anyone I knew, but I also tried as hard as I could to be a regular guy and often succeeded. Nevertheless, when I finally left for college, I breathed a long sigh of relief, one that lasted for months.

Looking back, I understand that it was not simply my homosexuality that made me dissatisfied with life in my hometown. Homosexual or heterosexual, many people are not cut out for suburban gracious living. I wanted to express myself in ways that were impossible to reconcile with the calm life of that town. But what I eventually discovered was that all the "unusual" things I did—going *away* to college, not coming home to work afterward, not marrying a hometown girl, not keeping up contacts with old friends and acquaintances—could be accepted, if not understood. Yet homosexuality, which I had encountered and explored in New York, could in no way be countenanced in my town. The people of middle America feel they have to draw the line somewhere to protect their way of life, and homosexuality is definitely on the other side of that line.

When I was a child, I was occasionally called "sissy" or "fairy." I was by no means an outstanding athlete, but that was not the reason for the remarks. They usually came when I was studying too hard or too obviously. Children are remarkably successful at incorporating the attitudes of adults around them. When I realized that what I enjoyed the most was despised or ignored, I decided to get out as soon as possible. If I had realized there was such a thing as homosexuality, I probably would have worked even harder to fit in. I might not have left, and that would have been a tragedy, for I would have suffocated myself.

Now my way of life will confront the people there with an ultimate assault on their beliefs. Most of them are kind, exemplary citizens. But I think others, as in any small town, would be so outraged by forthright advocacy of what they see as a threat that they would react with fear, bitterness, perhaps even violence. It has been known to happen. I do not want to subject my relatives, especially the children, to that. So I decided to change my name.

I talked over this decision with my mother. She was torn between a genuine pride that I was going to write a book (any book!) and an equally genuine fear of the unknown possible reaction of people in the town. Not for her sake, but for her children. She likes her neighbors, trusts them, admires some of them. But she was afraid of their reactions to a subject that shocked even her; she certainly was not yet ready to discuss my homosexuality with my sisters. She didn't want me to, and she did not want them to find out about it from strangers to whom homosexuality was either a joke or a crime. I understand and respect her fears, because they are grounded in reality.

The editor of this book wanted to put a picture on the dust jacket. I at first resisted, partly because of my desire to avoid hassles for my family and partly because I was a little worried about being used to sell the book. But two things became apparent. People at home could only recognize and label me by my old name. They hadn't *seen* me for years.

And it is important, I realized, that readers have somebody to identify with when they read the book; it's important that they know that I have long hair and a mustache—not that long hair and a mustache make me any more interesting, but that the readers thus might feel a little more communication with another gay person. I remember walking home from school one day with a friend, when I was eleven or twelve. We passed a very well-kept white house, set back from the street in the midst of several leafy trees. My friend told me that a fairy lived in that house. I never heard about that from anyone else, and I never saw the fairy. I never knew if he was young or old, nice or evil. But I always remembered that a fairy lived in that particular house. The label was enough.

I believe that homosexuality is a positive, constructive, totally viable life style. I really believe that being a homosexual anywhere is all right. I also know that you can be a homosexual openly in a large city and freely explore many different possibilities with a minimum of hassle. But to be openly homosexual, or even to be associated with homosexuality in a small town, is to invite disaster. You will be a laughingstock at best, and it is likely that you will encounter prosecution by the law or worse. If I were not around as the object of possible outrage, it could happen that my family would suffer in my place. That such an absurd state of affairs can exist is a primary reason for this book.

It is not enough that homosexuals be tolerated by liberals in large cities. It is not enough that a few laws be changed and their significance promptly forgotten. Homosexuals should be able to lead free lives wherever they want to. There should be nothing wrong with anyone's son, brother, or even father being a homosexual, if he is able to handle his life. Homosexuals are as well equipped—and perhaps better equipped—to handle their lives as are heterosexuals, particularly after senseless prejudices against homosexuality have been erased.

I wondered if I was copping out by changing my name. I had thought about the matter for weeks, and I had decided to use my real father's name instead of my stepfather's. No matter what my name is, I reasoned, the book would get the same response; the most important problem was certainly what was in the book, rather than who wrote it. If I were, say, George Plimpton or Norman Mailer trying to hide my identity while writing about a hot topic, that would make a difference. But this is my first book, and the emphasis is on the experiences in homosexuality that produced the book, rather than my personal life and development. To most readers, I hoped, the most important thing about me would not be my name: it would be that I am openly and proudly a homosexual.

And there is an extra, unexpected bonus I hadn't even considered. When a gay person takes on a new name, there can be a deeply satisfying symbolism. Like most of the others who have done so, I did it to protect my family. But I did not simply pick out a pseudonym. I am now John Murphy, and that new identity is liberating. Part of the thrust behind gay liberation is dissatisfaction with the traditional concept of the family. Men and women in America are expected to marry and become parents. The further away from this norm one strays, the more one will suffer for it. Taking a new name is a small but concrete step toward destroying the concept of family, which could have stifled me, as it has so many.

I love my family. I don't blame them or hold them responsible for my homosexuality any more than a heterosexual would for his sexuality. I do not feel obligated to them. We are close because we want to be. There is no worry that I will disgrace the family name, partly because I have dropped it. Nor do I still worry about their inability to recognize my homosexuality. They are fair and sensible people, and they will be able to adjust. What does bother me is that these fears exist at all. I have been homosexual

nearly all of my conscious life. I have had overt homosexual experiences for about five years. I have been openly
homosexual for perhaps a year and a half. And I am still discovering the multitude of ways by which the straight world
makes the lives of all homosexuals painful, while, most of
the time, remaining completely unconscious of the pain
inflicted.

• • •

This pain and confusion can come from anyone—family,
professional counselors who should know better, even friends.
As I was finishing the first draft of this book, a girl I had
known at college visited me with her husband. She is a
computer expert; he is a teacher going for his doctorate.
Although she and I had been close friends at school, we
hadn't really talked for a long time.

We exchanged greetings when they arrived; they hadn't
met the man I live with, so there was another little flurry
of introductions, nervous laughter, and tentative inquiries
about what exactly he was doing with *his* life. We told each
other about people from school we had seen lately; because
I had known Kathy much longer than her husband, Joe, we
knew exactly what kind of juicy items would interest each
other. After exhausting that, we all compared notes on the
weather in New York City and their present home, a university town in upstate New York. We agreed that it certainly
is nice to be in the country in the spring.

There was a lull in the conversation. Finally Kathy asked
me how my book was going. I said fine—my usual answer.
Sometimes I felt as if I had inadvertently let it be known
that I had bursitis, or some sort of allergy: I probably should
have kept my affliction to myself, but, since I had broad-
casted it to the world, I should be prepared to field questions
about it.

There was another short pause. Somebody yawned. Then Joe, whom I did not know well, asked me exactly how I was organizing the book. I started to describe what I wanted it to be: one person's feelings and experiences as he explored the homosexual liberation movement and its background. I didn't think it could be in any way definitive, but it could be true, which I think very few books about homosexuality today are.

Joe kept zeroing in: Was it going to be philosophical, or historical, or political . . . ? I said no, it's going to be personal. I felt that somehow most of the problems homosexuals have today are a result of their lack of self-identity. They have had plenty of histories of homosexuality, philosophical defenses of and attacks on it, psychological analyses of what is wrong with homosexuals (or, much more rarely, what is right with them) . But homosexuality has always been treated as a problem, something to be triumphed over or gotten around. The gay liberation movement, of which this book would be one product, asserts that homosexuality should not be a problem, that it is instead a powerful and creative force that should be recognized and encouraged. Kathy sat quietly, looking from her husband to me with a worried frown.

Then Joe changed his line of questioning. Did I find that my thinking had changed as I worked on the book, that it had even assumed a new direction? I remember thinking that he must be doing some writing on his own, because he was talking about problems I had gone over and over as I wrote. I answered yes, my thought had changed. I had started by attempting to provide a coherent approach to gay liberation, showing how homosexuals needed such a movement, and that this movement could affect our lives. But the longer I worked, the more I realized that I wasn't describing a set of clear-cut principles or a series of easily charted events. I was trying to figure out a new way of looking at my own life, my whole life, not just the sexual aspects of it. And

I was still trying to generalize—a trait I distrusted, yet one almost impossible to avoid when discussing the lives of homosexuals. Or of any group.

I tried to show how the most important part of the book would be the communication of feelings, not principles. He looked at me blankly, and I started again. Homosexuals have certain feelings in common in this country; the most pervasive and acute until now have been guilt and shame at being something that was feared and despised by straight society. Some can handle this, but it has crippled millions of others. To live as an invisible man is incredibly painful. Joe still looked blank. I certainly didn't seem invisible to him, he said.

Jim, the man I live with, started to explain how the gay liberation movement was basically an attempt to find a new way of living for people who were tired of and disgusted by the old way. There were alternatives for homosexuals that we had never been told about, just as straight people were discovering that there were new alternatives for them. But what must be understood was that homosexuals weren't going to be kept down any longer. They weren't going to live as "sick" creatures or hide their sexuality and pose as straight to avoid trouble.

Kathy had listened to the men talk until then, nodding occasionally, a perfect picture of a dutiful wife. When she finally spoke, she asked what all this would mean to people like her. My first response was that it really didn't have anything to do with her. But I realized that, even though she was straight, she was still trying to figure out what to do about this new determination that she had never seen before in me or anyone else.

She talked about how she was perhaps old-fashioned because she was family-oriented. She had come from a large family, and she wanted one of her own. But, if everyone was free to pursue his own sexual interests, if there was no longer an ideal of producing good, new people, what would happen to people like her and Joe? Would there still be families? Or would there be homosexual families, or would straight people and gay people marry and produce children, or what?

Now it was my turn to be puzzled. Her questions seemed so naïve. The need to propagate the race was ludicrous in the midst of starving cities and nations. But then I realized that she really had not understood me, and this was because I was speaking as a homosexual. I could envision some sort of new, changed social order where homosexuality would be free and open. She could not. She had too much to lose—her husband, her future family, everything she had always assumed was true. She said that this part of my life was foreign to her, that she had never been able to imagine what it was like.

She had good reason to be confused and cautious, because there was no way she could ever really understand except by being a homosexual. I tried to tell her that the movement, and even this book, was not aimed at straight people like her; it was not supposed to educate straight people so they could understand and accept homosexuals. I wanted to show what I had discovered about myself as a homosexual and try to communicate something of that sense of freedom to other homosexuals. If it bothered or disgusted or scared straight people, they would have to pull themselves together and adjust. We certainly have been adjusting to them long enough.

Joe asked me if I had reached any concrete conclusions. The conversation was really beginning to disturb Kathy, but I felt that I had to get the point across once and for all. I mentioned one thing I had finally decided to propose as a sensible demand. This was a change in education. I said that, because homosexuality was a fact of life that children start hearing references to at an early age, it should be discussed as an acceptable life style in any kind of sex education program, at any age. I thought of my sisters as I said this and

how our awkward situation could have been eased. I don't
know what Kathy thought of, but she paled and swallowed
hard. The conversation about homosexuality was over.

That night, after they left, I thought for a long time about
our conversation. It had shown me more clearly than ever
the widening gap between even the most liberal straight
person and a homosexual who is trying to assert his own
identity. I had had similar encounters before, even with
other homosexuals. These were usually older people who
were puzzled about what exactly it was that gay liberation
wanted. How do you tell somebody that you want a new way
to live, that you are tired of always playing with rules where
you lose?

The image of an angry homosexual demanding anything
terrifies most straight people and a lot of gays. It has never
happened before, certainly not in this country. But that is
what is going on now. Homosexuals have been working for
nearly twenty years in organized groups to gain their civil
rights—working to repeal legislation against themselves, to
protect gay employees, to stop police abuse. But they have
worked within the American system; they have tried to blend
in, to be acceptable to straight people of good will like Kathy
and Joe. Angry homosexuals have surfaced only in the last
few years. They encounter hostility on all sides, and they
return it. But they make things happen and change. It is
unfortunate that intelligent, sympathetic straight people and
even many homosexuals who want to live in the straight
world cannot understand radical homosexuals. But that cannot influence the demands or behavior of these radicals.
They are acting out of their need, and it is up to other
people to realize that visible homosexuality, as a proud life
style, is here for good.

· · ·

The temptation to compare the gay liberation movement with the struggles of other oppressed groups is very strong. But, like each of these other struggles, this one must be judged on its own merits, not just as part of the massive upheaval we are all going through. The special problems surrounding homosexuality are manifold and concrete. Homosexuals remain the least visible minority group. They also cooperate to the greatest extent in their own oppression. Attitudes toward homosexuality have been intensely hostile in most countries for centuries. Any attempt to confront and change these attitudes will probably be met with intense resistance, both from those who benefit by these prejudices and from those who are discriminated against.

The homosexual liberation movement is essentially a young cause. Individuals of all ages are within the movement, but the greatest impetus in the last few years has come from young women and men. Attitudes of most older people I have talked to ranged from outright hostility to the patronizing approval bestowed on someone who is working at something that will keep him out of trouble.

The sharply defined groups within the movement are often in fierce competition; but what they share is their members' acknowledgment of their own primary identity as *homosexuals*. They feel that the attitude of America today threatens that identity, threatens them, and are therefore ready to use drastic measures for change. Many homosexuals wish to make a place for themselves in the established American order, to continue living in a "subculture" that has evolved primarily as a defensive device. Liberationists will usually define themselves as socially radical and, often, as politically radical; they thus place themselves in opposition to the conservative and reactionary, whether heterosexual or homosexual. The young in the movement, moreover, are impatient with their forerunners and are usually ready to escalate their activities at the slightest provocation. But we are all united in our determination to forge a place for ourselves in a new order.

This book is an account of one homosexual's emergence into that radicalism. As I told my straight friends, I can't claim to speak ultimately for anyone but myself. I do feel that my experiences are not without parallels in lives of other gay people. I have written about my experiences in New York City, and primarily about experiences with other men. Gay Liberation is a national movement and is spreading to other countries as well. Women are certainly as vital to it as men. I have limited myself to writing about what I know best, and even that has often been ferociously difficult. There are viewpoints and events and people I will perhaps slight or even pass over. Any inaccuracy or distortion is unintentional, the result of trying to get something important said as soon as possible. There will be many other books by and for gay people soon, and they will tell other parts of the story.

2 *learning and unlearning some hard terms*

BRAINWASHING OF GAY people begins at birth. It surrounds us like the air we breathe, so that most of the time we are not even aware of it. But, as the impact of the liberation movement grows, many of these myths and fallacies are finally being dispelled. People need to be re-educated. Therefore, the gay liberation movement has circulated pamphlets, flyers, and throwaways expressing its positions and demands; it has held thousands of meetings and staged numerous happenings. But the emphasis in most of these has either remained on the abstract level of theoretical statements or concerned the heated yet elusive emotions of spur-of-the-moment confrontations. These activities are crucial, but we also need personal statements that go into detail about the

23

oppression and liberation of individuals. To do this, we have to come to terms with the attitudes that we have inherited from families, friends, schools, the media, religion—the society we live in.

Any discussion of the gay world must unfortunately still start with a definition of terms. The myth of the post–World War II sexual revolution has fostered the notion that we can now speak openly about sex, that at last we can communicate about matters that were until now taboo, that we will all soon be all right because now we can tell the truth. But we have only begun to explore the possibilities and implications of sexuality; as a nation we find it easier to view sex on the movie screen than to confront it realistically in sex-education programs. The fevered atmosphere that permeates "singles" bars is hardly the result of any liberation or breakthrough; to many, it is a breakdown.

We are just beginning to develop a realistic sexual vocabulary that can relate sex to the rest of our lives. There are immense difficulties, moreover, in communication between homosexuals and heterosexuals, and among homosexuals themselves. Some short definitions of terms currently being used are necessary. These terms, like every other definition and judgment in the book, are admittedly personal and biased and are subject to revision.

The term homosexuality is commonly understood as referring to sexual activities—physical and emotional, repressed and overt—between members of the same sex. The root word *homo* in Greek means "the same"; in Latin, however, *homo* means "man." To avoid casting the whole issue in the male mold that dominates so much of our thought, many women prefer the term "lesbian" (from the Greek island Lesbos, home of the poet Sappho) . Thus they eliminate the implied reference to the male who has oppressed so many women, particularly lesbians. I use the term homosexual in referring to both men and women, but I realize that the connotation is unavoidably male. And perhaps that is the most honest stance I can take. I *know* the experiences I have faced as a male homosexual: I cannot presume to speak for women.

The word gay, adopted by the gay liberation movement's various organizations, seems to be an ideal solution to these problems of terminology. Gay—like faggot, queer, dyke, queen—was originally a term of abuse. It has been seized on, however, as an affirmation of the positive aspects of homosexuality. "Gay is good." "Say it loud, gay and proud." "Two, four, six, eight, gay is just as good as straight." All these have become standard chants at movement demonstrations. But they show a new determination to live honestly. To the straight world, we may be queers flaunting our hang-ups. To ourselves, we are finally living in the open. The old names, mentioned above, can no longer be endured as epithets; we have earned the right to use them among ourselves if we want to, but we are not going to be dismissed as "sick" fags and dykes.

Concepts of the homosexual, of homosexuality as a life style, of the threat to heterosexuals from homosexuality—all are formed by society, with heterosexuality as the standard by which every person's "deviant" behavior is judged. If this seems a rather vague point, perhaps a quick practical demonstration will help. Think of your brother (or cousin, or daughter, or aunt) becoming a homosexual. Think of this quickly, what it would mean to them and to you. Now think of them becoming a heterosexual. More relaxing, right? The idea of someone *becoming* a heterosexual is laughable, because heterosexuality is more or less natural, or at least more normal, right? Heterosexual is what almost everybody is anyway, right? Wrong.

Homosexuality is thought of by enlightened, liberal heterosexuals as basically a psychological "problem," a sort of infirmity that they hope can be cured or ignored. Psychologists tell us that there are homosexual elements in everyone's nature during childhood; they also say that heterosexuals outgrow these impulses. Homosexuals, then, are simply cases of arrested development, according to this school of thought; as they become more mature, they should straighten out— that is, be cured. Unfortunately, these views totally negate the lives of several million people.

So let us try to define the situation by actualities. Women *do* get into bed with men and have intercourse. Women also get into bed with other women and have intercourse. And men get into bed with other men and have intercourse. When we move within and between these sectors, we don't wear little changeable signs, like streetcars—"homosexual," "heterosexual," "bisexual." We simply function as sexual beings. All of us are potentially homosexual, heterosexual, bisexual. When we speak of ourselves as homosexual, we use a handy term, a sort of shorthand invented by a frightened straight world to protect its imaginary and real privileges. Like all labels, the term homosexuality can never do more than begin to signify the full range of our possibilities: the homosexual, woman and man, self-proclaimed and ashamed . . . also the homosexual that is a part of everyone . . . but not the exclusively heterosexual, because no such creature can exist.

•   •   •

The concept of sex roles has assumed a terrifyingly dispro-portionate value in America. We have taken the basic sexual tensions that characterize most societies and institutionalized them, overlaying the whole structure with our uniquely American commercialism. Sex is our most powerful selling tool, and the male-female sexual stereotypes are the key to moving the goods, whether they be cars, margarine, vaginal deodorants, or cigars. Our advertising reflects the basic values we attribute to the ideal man and woman; the values go much deeper, of course, but they are codified in advertising as in a religion.

Sexism is a descriptive term for the attitudes about our sexuality that force us into unrealistic, often deadly, positions and roles. Sexism is the mentality that equates the size of a man's penis or a woman's breasts with his or her desirability and worth. Sexism equates being a woman with being a mother and being a man with being a provider. Thus an American woman who does not marry must be in some way unfulfilled (despite the disclaimers of people like Helen Gurley Brown); a married woman who chooses not to have children is somehow "selfish." Sexism is the double standard, the still widespread compulsion of men to seduce and conquer women, proving their masculinity, and yet still expect to marry a virgin who will remain faithful. Sexism is the reason women are notoriously underpaid in jobs where they compete with men, doing the same work for less money. Sexism is the traditional belief that women are and should be weaker than men. The ultimate expression of sexism is rape.

Men would seem to suffer less from sexism. But they must also play their roles; they also are trapped by expectations that are humanly impossible to fulfill. Men are expected to be stronger, more self-reliant, more sensible than women. When a man meets a woman who is reasonably intelligent and sure of herself, he can too often drive himself into a frenzy of meaningless competition. Although men are expected to be the protectors of women, there is a concurrent tradition, prevalent in all social classes, to victimize women by using them as sex objects. If a man feels deeply for a woman, he has "fallen" in love with her. He is a little foolish, perhaps even stupid, because a woman has him under her thumb. For a woman to fall in love with a man is only natural, of course; it's only expected that a woman would let her emotions run away with her.

Thus, in the heterosexual world, men and women are trapped. Women are supposed to be at once sexy and virtuous, dependent and capable of handling a home and, ideally, a job; they should be romantic and sentimental, yet psychologically perceptive enough to understand the problems of their men. A man must be aggressive and demanding, yet remain a nice guy; he must suppress any softness he may feel and adhere to a code of masculinity that equates a genial *machismo* with real achievement.

Homosexuals are part of the heterosexual world; they have usually been raised by heterosexuals, and they live in a culture that is heterosexually dominated. Thus, many homosexuals choose to adopt sexist attitudes created by heterosexuals; their situation as an invisible minority creates a whole set of particular problems, however. The way homosexuals relate to one another is popularly—and falsely—characterized as a sort of mirror image of traditional male-female relationships —that is, as a power play. There is thought to be a dominant (read masculine) and a submissive (read feminine) partner in each relationship, each displaying the concomitant behavior patterns. Despite the irrelevance of these roles to many homosexual relationships, many other homosexuals accept and even cling to such stereotypes. Thus the popular picture of the homosexual couple living a parody of heterosexual married life—"wife" in a frilly apron, protected by a brusque but lovable "husband" (although, because these are homosexuals, even the husband must be a little "feminine").

Sexism is expressed in every destructive aspect of homosexuality—the guilt-ridden promiscuity, the pressures against proclaiming one's homosexuality openly, the fascination with appearances that too often demonstrates a lack of thought-out values. The extremely masculine and feminine stances that many homosexuals adopt are individual responses to the demands of a sexist society; the ultimate extensions of these demands are the leather-clad motorcyclist and the drag queen. Individuals are driven into behaving like the super-man or the quintessential female to survive in a highly competitive and destructive sexual contest. If to be masculine is to be strong or to be feminine is to be wanted, then these stances are self-protective roles rather than genuine life styles. (Note that the two extreme stances given as examples above were both applicable to males. A woman's situation is even more limited. She may perhaps be judged too masculine, but never too feminine.)

One of the major purposes of this book is to condemn any attempt to characterize relationships based on stereotyped sexual roles. It is imperative that homosexuals begin, as women already have, to cast off oppressive sexual definitions, both those created by society and those created by homosexuals themselves. Homosexuals must actively *choose* the ways in which they relate to each other and to the straight world. This personal process of choosing is the first and most vital step in creating a new kind of freedom that can change our dying culture.

• • •

That the United States can and does oppress individuals and other nations has become a central concern among thoughtful people in the last decade. As our smoldering heritage of racism exploded on our television screens and in our cities, many whites realized that black Americans, who had been oppressed for hundreds of years, were now demanding redress for their torture and mutilation. Oppression became real to the oppressor and was terrifying.

But the simple recognition that the problem of racism exists does not constitute a solution. And, as black-white tensions have grown, other problems have reared their troublesome heads. Women's liberation grew from a topic for Book-of-the-Month Club best sellers by women like Betty

Friedan and Caroline Bird, to a standard source of humor in news programs and comedians' monologues, finally to the status of inclusion in the lists of ills besetting our nation that periodically appear in the editorials of serious newspapers. Women were talking about their oppression, and they were beginning to act against it.

To the American liberal male, who was only beginning to adjust to his newly discovered racism, the charge of sexism was an amusing, if somewhat annoying, diversion. The response of most men (and many women) to the challenges of women's liberation was "How in God's name are *you* oppressed?" Answers were not long in coming, from women of every political, economic, and social stratum. Women were tired of being abused, underpaid, overworked, raped, ignored, economically exploited by an advertising economy, and intellectually nullified by those to whom they were expected to dedicate their lives. But it is not my intention to describe here the real and terrible ordeal of women in America; the evidence is all around us. And I do not believe any man could ever understand and speak for an oppressed woman as truly as she herself could.

The sexual balance of a nation, like that of an individual, is fragile. Disruption in one sphere can rapidly lead to disorder in many spheres. As blacks demanded to be heard, as women seized their rights and abandoned their privileges, a new group began to speak of their oppression. And, if the rage of women against their plight was at first a source of humor, this group could be counted on to provide a veritable laugh riot. For these people were homosexuals.

An individual's reaction to charges of oppression of homosexuals will correspond directly to his conception of what a homosexual is. Blacks, women, the poor—all these people are highly visible. If society agrees that they indeed do have legitimate grievances, these people can be recognized as oppressed. They can be easily classified by their physical appearance, if nothing else. But homosexuals are most often *not* visible, particularly to the straight world. The popular stereotypes of effeminate men, lisping and walking poodles, or "mannish" female gym teachers are caricatures of one element of homosexuality. These caricatures make fools of the people they parody, depriving them of the dignity they deserve. Moreover, these people are made to bear the weight of representing all homosexuals. Like Aunt Jemima or Blondie, the caricatures may have originally had some validity; now they are cruel and stupid jokes. But as yet there has been no outcry against these popular caricatures of homosexuals, as there has been against the legendary dumb blonde or Stepin Fetchit. Perhaps this is because very few people in the straight world want to know about the real world of homosexuals. They prefer to laugh at a joke, rather than face the truth about others—and themselves.

Daily I meet new people and see old friends. Many are completely unaware that I am a homosexual, and others simply prefer to ignore the facts. Living in New York, with its large gay population, there are occasions when I and a straight acquaintance run into a highly visible homosexual friend of mine—one of those individuals who are perhaps extremely vocal, sometimes outrageously dressed, often acidly humorous, and quite possibly brilliant. As my two spheres of acquaintances intersected more frequently, I became increasingly dismayed at my straight friends' reactions. Those who know of my homosexuality respond exactly as those who do not know—they attempt to ignore my gay friends or quickly make a humorous (and usually extremely disparaging) reference to the odd characters I know. I discovered something that should have been obvious for years: heterosexual men *never* relate easily to visibly homosexual men. Moreover, they ignore homosexuality that is not visible. Because I was not an obvious homosexual, they could relate to me. But, if I ever crossed that invisible line, I would quickly and surely be cut adrift from the heterosexual world.

Thus, I have received the greatest insights into my own

oppression when I confronted friends with the fact of my homosexuality. It is then that some of my life's deepest experiences—intimate physical and emotional relationships with other men—are denied by these friends, who may not be friends at all. In a liberal, enlightened, kind, and always intelligent way, they tell me that my life is perhaps diseased, at best misdirected, and definitely abnormal.

When I told a male friend that I was thinking of writing a book, he was excited and curious and asked what it was about. Summoning up my courage—for it is always hard to speak of your personal life to someone who is not expecting any genuine insights—I told him it was to be on homosexual liberation.

Silence. Finally, "Well . . . how are you going to find out about it? I mean . . . what is your point of view?"

"From the inside, I guess. From the viewpoint of somebody who wanted to make it with men and did it."

More silence. Then, quite cheerfully, "That's fantastic. Really, I had no idea. I mean, you don't even *look* like a homosexual."

I found myself suddenly bitter. What in hell was I supposed to look like, anyway? And why was he so glad that I didn't *look* like a homosexual? What about what I actually *did*? I suddenly realized how humiliating it must be to hear that one doesn't look Jewish. It isn't funny.

This happened many times, but one more example should suffice. The topic came up when I was talking about future plans with a beautiful and intelligent young woman in a cafe. When I said I was working on a book on homosexual liberation—because I was a homosexual—she was quiet for a moment and then leaned across the table and touched my hand. "It's all right. Really," she whispered. She was very sweet and serious, as if I had just told her that I was going to need a lobotomy or die of tuberculosis. I didn't know whether to laugh or to shout at her. Why shouldn't it be all right? There was nothing I needed reassurance about from her, and her patronizing became even more infuriating as I realized that she was not even aware of anything wrong in what she was saying.

Perhaps these examples of oppression are overly subtle. Nobody has called me a faggot on the street . . . yet. But I have always been aware that I was somehow being hurt. These forms of oppression that I am constantly discovering fascinate me, because they explain some of that pain. I have realized that most heterosexuals don't understand the ways they oppress homosexuals. They had better begin to understand, however, and soon, for that oppression is about to be destroyed and, with it, the world that they know.

Homosexual men and women begin to feel their oppression as soon as they realize that they want to be close to other people of their own sex. This falls outside the rules of conduct in America, perhaps more obviously for men. An American boy does certain things: He plays ball; he will—ideally —drive a car fast and well; he wants to be at least as strong as his father; he dislikes little girls but must be nice to them. An American boy does not play with dolls; if he is normal, he is not gentle; he does not—God forbid—dance or paint, at least until he is into his teens, and then only if his parents are extremely enlightened. He does not ever affectionately touch any boy in a sexual manner. He can, however, fantasize about the girl next door. He is nominally supposed to feel guilty about these dirty thoughts, but it is understood that every boy goes through these stages, and it is hoped that these feelings will be replaced by a tender regard for the "right girl" someday. Thus any sexual fantasizing or experimentation with other boys is a straying away from his rightful role; it can happen, of course, but he should forget about it as soon as possible.

But unbidden thoughts usually do not go away. A boy does not choose what he thinks about; he simply thinks. And, as he grows older, he often becomes horrified at his own thoughts, because, in the world outside his mind, he can find no correlative to what he thinks. He may want and need, in a sexual sense, friends who are boys growing into men like himself. But the American culture pushes him into a fierce competition for the female, a hunt where he is supposed to defeat all others and gain the ultimate prize—the beautiful, good, sexy girl who will satisfy all his needs. Girls become mere objects in this search for perfection, and the young homosexual often finds himself in competition with men and women.

The fact that no such female perfection exists outside our popular imagination makes very little difference to a boy who has been raised on *Playboy's* ultimate eighteen-year-old beauty, high school proms, Raquel Welch (or Marilyn Monroe or even Jean Harlow) films, television commercials, and even "serious" literature (D. H. Lawrence, Henry Miller, Norman Mailer, and too many others—see Kate Millett's *Sexual Politics*) that all picture women as sometimes intuitive, sometimes sexy, but basically dumb creatures.

There is no escape today for a young man who does not wish to go that route with women, unless he is prepared to stand outside American social and cultural tradition. If, in addition, he likes and respects other men to the point where he wishes to be sexually intimate with them, he must be prepared to be called, variously, a homosexual, a homo, a fairy, a queer, a faggot, a pansy, a poof, a cocksucker. He cannot simply be a man. He must have a label for the rest of the world's convenience, and that label must be derogatory. He can retreat into a strictly homosexual life, where he will face another set of labels. But there, at least, he will find a certain measure of acceptance and peace. Those who can't or won't make such a retreat now face the prospect of a lonely and hidden life, if they give in to their homosexuality, or a hideously meaningless frustration, if they don't.

Readers, particularly heterosexual readers, will protest that I am generalizing too much. "Homosexuality is a very complicated problem; it is dangerous to oversimplify; anyway, we are just beginning to learn about these things." But it is maddening to wait for all the facts to be in when you are trying to discover what is true about your life. I know *my* life; I know what *I* have suffered and enjoyed. What I am just beginning to realize is the extent to which the most natural and generous impulses of myself and men I have known have been denied by those nearest to us; these impulses have been so mangled that we have often ended up imitating the sad and grotesque caricature that straight society sees as *the homosexual*—a caricature no one could ever live up to.

I have not yet mentioned the most obvious and blatant forms of oppression; perhaps overoptimistically, I still hope these injustices will soon be recognized and condemned universally. Homosexuals are daily attacked, beaten, and robbed, sometimes simply because they are homosexuals, sometimes by hustlers who are terrified of admitting their own homosexuality. Robbery or blackmail of a homosexual victim has recently become a popular "weird" theme in crime fiction and films, where once again the homosexual is ridiculed and made to look stupid and pathetic. Homosexuals—and police —have known for years of the terrifying ferocity that accompanies these attacks; this ferocity arises out of the genuine threat that homosexuals pose to aggressive heterosexual maleness. Like the rape of women, the physical assaults on homosexuals are not simply criminal acts; they are the convulsions of a diseased society, which must change.

There are also constant, infuriating hassles in day-to-day life. Homosexuals are fired from jobs when their sexual preferences are known by anyone outside a small circle of friends. This is not restricted to highly publicized government jobs requiring security clearance; it happens from the corner grocery store to Wall Street law firms. Homosexuality is classed as a mental illness and therefore grounds for deferment from the army and dishonorable discharge for those already serving. Ironically, this has proved to be a blessing for the homosexual men who, like so many other Americans, bitterly oppose the entire American bureaucratic-military operation. In a situation of overpopulation, homosexuals, like all other single people, still are discriminated against by an economic system based on taxation that favors the nuclear family—the larger, the better. Two men may find it extremely difficult to rent an apartment together, even in large cities, if there is any taint of acknowledged homosexuality in their relationship. Lesbian women encounter even more of the difficulties that confront all women—unwanted solicitations from men in public places, attempted victimization by men in the business world, and worst of all, the constant negative evaluations made about unmarried women and their supposed frustrations, frigidity, and ugliness.

Yet the most irritating, deadening, and poignant denials occur in what may seem to be the smallest matters. America is a land of idealized lovers strolling down lanes hand in hand; but there had better be only two of them, and they'd better be a man and a woman. I see young men and women daily, holding hands, kissing in public, just generally making out. And until recently I felt benevolent; it was good that someone could express affection, even if they often looked like they didn't really mean it, even if their displays seemed meant to convince the world rather than to please each other. One night several months ago, a friend was walking with me toward my subway stop; he leaned over and kissed me good night—on the mouth, in public. I was embarrassed, angry, afraid. Even if it was late, someone might see. They might think that we were . . . what? Queer? But we are. And I enjoyed kissing him. Men and women could do it when they wanted to, even in public. Why couldn't we? Why couldn't we do whatever we wanted? There was no reason. I had always been told "no," but that didn't make sense anymore.

• • •

Several terms that will appear throughout this book may at first sound like agitprop jargon to the uninitiated. These terms have evolved out of countless hours of discussion and have gathered connotations that make them extremely meaningful for anyone interested in understanding the homosexual liberation movement. "Consciousness" is one such word —an old term that has acquired new and specific meaning.

Consciousness of one's existence as a homosexual is an awareness of your basic needs and rights, how these factors are related to your homosexuality, and how the world responds (and could respond) to your homosexuality. The term is really a succinct description of a constant process of self-recognition, a process that also encompasses a growing recognition of how you interact with the people around you. Again, these concepts are perhaps best explained by personal references.

Until recently, I had taken many of my attitudes about sexuality for granted; I had never thought out clearly or defined them. As I became painfully aware of my personal need for a more realistic approach to homosexuality, I was also becoming involved with an extraordinary group of men and women who are active, vocal homosexuals. I heard them articulate, for the first time in my life, ideas to which I could at last relate directly. I did not have to translate these ideas so that they could apply to me as well as to heterosexuals. These people were talking about *my* experiences, and I suddenly became aware of many things—things that I had taken for granted, things that could be changed, things that were hurting me.

Sexuality in America seems to have passed from Puritanism, the result of hundreds of years of Western European moral domination, directly to an often cynical era of self-gratification, personal detachment, and objectification of other people. Homosexuals had been forced to create a closed, self-protective, and isolated subculture, and these destructive processes could grow much more quickly in an atmosphere akin to the hot-house milieu of *The Boys in the Band*. Personally, my consciousness of myself as a homosexual has changed to the point where I can finally see myself as part of that culture, which I had feared and avoided yet which was a constant source of fascination. At the same time I realized that I would never really *be* one of the boys in the band, that by accepting my sexuality I had made a personal breakthrough to a new kind of freedom.

I could do what I wanted, and it did not make any difference what anyone else thought about it. The responsibilities entailed by this simple realization, however, shook me badly. I thought I had already settled these matters in adolescence, but I had not. I had always separated my sexual life from any areas of daily concern, since the disapproval of others could obviously do me a lot of harm. Now, I finally realized that going to bed with men could bring me closer to some people and alienate me from others who were repelled by my behavior; but there was no reason for any taboos or condemnation, because there was nothing wrong with what I was doing.

And, almost simultaneously with this knowledge that I was doing nothing wrong, I saw that some other people were. I had been told that my sexuality was wrong. I had been admonished and threatened by a lot of people who told me that wanting to touch men was wrong, although wanting to touch women was all right. I was . . . oppressed! I was being kept down by *them*, by the same people who were keeping down the blacks, students, the poor, women. My consciousness was slowly, excruciatingly being raised. And I started to wonder what my oppressors were afraid of.

The political aspects of homosexuality are difficult to define and more difficult to act on; yet they exist, and they profoundly affect every homosexual's life. This is the area strangely enough, where homosexual liberation encounters the most resistance among homosexuals themselves. When I started attending meetings of a group known as the Gay Liberation Front, I tried to explain to an old friend how I suddenly found myself recognizing the extent of my oppression as a homosexual (although I avoided the actual word "oppression," because it has no meaning as yet in the jargon of the establishment gay world). My friend listened politely, if not attentively. "It sounds very good," he commented. "But there are babies starving in Biafra. They need a cure for cancer. . . . There *are* some things that should get a higher priority, I think." I disagreed, but I didn't have any counterargument; I felt a little shamefaced because of the obvious seriousness of his remarks.

When I discussed the incident with some other men in the movement and did some thinking by myself, I reached some conclusions about my friend that could be applied to me also. Like him, I was a product of the middle class; like him, I was relatively well educated, relatively well read; like him, I could not be readily spotted as a homosexual by straight people; and, like him, I had not been openly abused or berated by the straight world—at least not since childhood, when I had rapidly learned to hide my sexuality. I was only too glad to accede to him when he denied the importance of our homosexuality. Although homosexuality was a major element in both our lives, we rarely discussed it openly. Rather, we gossiped about the actions of other people or occasionally tried to express the confusion of a particularly unhappy emotional involvement. We didn't talk about the over-all social and political significance of homosexuality, and this was because there didn't seem to *be* any over-all significance. When I wasn't thinking specifically about my sex life, homosexuality didn't exist for me. And, like my friend, I was glad for that. Out of sight, out of mind, and therefore out of trouble.

But, as I started to explore seriously the implications of my past experiences, as I talked to men and women in the movement, homosexuals outside of it, and even straight people, I realized that I was indeed a homosexual twenty-four hours a day. Through psychotherapy I had learned at least to be wary of placing labels on myself and my behavior; by my personal definitions, I was not and am not homosexual or heterosexual, not gay or straight, not sick or healthy; I remain just plain old me. But society looked at what I did and labeled me quickly and permanently. And it quickly translated these labels into bases for action.

According to these labels, I was sick. This is not an over-statement; to be homosexual in a heterosexually dominated culture is to be considered unhealthy, a cause for concern. A few self-acknowledged homosexuals may be accepted, but they are viewed as anomalies, freaks. The way of life I share with my brothers should be hidden, according to these rules. If it is not hidden, it will be at best ignored, more likely ridiculed, and possibly even persecuted. Oppression may be blatant and cruel or urbane and sophisticated, but it does exist. Through no fault of our own, we have been condemned to the status of members of a minority group. In a country where the majority rules, a minority is to be pitied, patron-ized, exploited, and, above all, kept a minority.

Homosexuals are supposed to keep their homosexuality a secret. Their most intimate contacts will usually be with other homosexuals. And thus the subculture thrives—a cul-ture kept beneath the regular culture. Special codes and ways of behavior evolve within to ensure survival and perhaps even a little pleasure. Suppliers move in, focusing on the areas of greatest sensitivity. Bars, private clubs, baths, sex magazines, specially designed clothing—all are used to inten- sify the experience of the homosexual within the gay ghetto. The homosexual's life style is condemned by the straight world, but he is not allowed to leave his ghetto and openly retain his homosexual identity; if he wants to get out, he has to pass for straight. It is interesting to note that popular opinion no longer requires blacks to adopt white life styles in order to be accepted as equals; and the prospect of women adopting male life styles has sent most of the nation into a paranoid frenzy. But homosexuals must pass.

Many people are unhappy with this kind of oppression. They want something new, and they are determined to get it. They constitute a potentially enormous revolutionary force. For we—I now include myself among these men and women—are not merely interested in being accepted. We don't need new bureaucracies to make a government more responsive to our "needs." Nor will we be content with new political entities created in the name of social revolution if they embody the same old repressive attitudes. We intend to restructure the most basic attitudes toward sexuality, the importance of the individual, the function of the family. We are going to try to make a *total* revolution.

3 *queer books*

W<small>E CAN DRAW</small> up long lists about how society oppresses homosexuals, but specific incidents make the truth more immediate. Some of the most obvious—yet least examined— manifestations of homosexual oppression occur in literature. Besides psychiatry, this is the only area of American culture where homosexuality is examined in depth. Until recently, it has also been the only platform for public statements by self-acknowledged homosexuals. An examination of American popular literature as experienced by one homosexual shows a frightening range of attitudes toward homosexuality —almost all negative. The antihomosexuality in these books is a prime example of what has made the gay liberation movement necessary and inevitable.

When a boy is curious about sex, he can get detailed information about every aspect of sexual activity, psychological, biological, or literary-erotic, at his neighborhood drugstore's paperback rack—if he is interested in heterosexuality. If a boy wants to learn anything about himself in relation to other males, he encounters a special set of problems. The ideal solution, of course, would be to discuss his feelings with a sympathetic and knowledgeable older person; unfortunately, the chances of encountering someone like that are extremely slim, due to the defensive reactions about frank discussions of sex common to most people in Western society. So the inquisitive young person will probably turn to books. If he has homosexual inclinations, the choice of books dealing with *his* sexual concerns are limited to a few serious "classics," some sensational popular novels, and pornography. Psychology texts—if he has the background to understand them—range from discussions of homosexuality as a form of pathology to a standard liberal acceptance of it as an expression of an individual's neurosis. These medical attitudes toward homosexuality, although sometimes in advance of public opinion, often do more harm than good simply because they usually view homosexuality as a medical matter—that is, as something that is wrong with you.

A discussion of the popular literature that deals with homosexuality cannot be definitive, because practically every novel, play, short story or poem that deals with sexual roles says something about out attitudes toward homosexuality, if only by pointedly ignoring it. Here, I will discuss what I have encountered as one reader who has used a voracious literary appetite in a hit-and-miss technique to cover as much material on homosexuality as possible. Actually, a hit-and-miss technique is practically the only possible way to approach social attitudes toward homosexuality in books available to the nonspecialist. Only a few serious books on psychological aspects of homosexuality are useful as background reading for the general reader, and these are usually distinguished by their marked distaste for homosexuals and homosexuality. Martin Hoffman's *The Gay World* is a notable exception. Although it tells homosexuals very little they do not already know about gay life, it is an ideal introduction for the straight person who may be interested in learning more about homosexuality. Hoffman's relatively unbiased approach concentrates on dealing with homosexuality as a form of personal expression that should be as viable as heterosexuality. Using books like his, homosexuals may soon assemble a long-needed body of works about homosexuality, which will become the basis for homosexual studies, past and present. Rather than being a subdivision of psychological investigation, this corpus would stand on its own merits, much like the newly discovered black literature and the works concerning women—both of which are now being re-evaluated.

Since early childhood, I have devoured books. Fortunately, my family and a few of my teachers encouraged this appetite for reading. I went to a Catholic grammar school, high school, and college, the last two run by those quintessential Catholics, the Jesuits. I received a strict, rather formal, education, somewhat out of the tradition of American public education. But I have found that the ways in which this specialized education affects my life and attitudes, in comparison with the effects of public education on others, differ less each year. I may have worn uniforms to class, and I may have been encouraged to say the rosary at home, but I have found that Catholic and public education share practically all of the same moral stances and sanctions, particularly regarding sexuality. The nuns were just a lot more colorful in describing the attendant dangers of sex.

Like every other child of the World War II years, I was raised on the Dick-and-Jane readers, which showed the ideal American family—a hard-working Father, a domestic sweetly

compliant Mother, and charming, chubby children, who
varied in age and sex from grade to grade. The life portrayed
in these books was lily-white and as straight as an arrow. No
matter that it corresponded to practically nothing that happened to anyone *I* knew; this was how it was supposed to be.
To supplement what I was supposed to be learning in elementary school, I grabbed whatever I could lay my hands on,
from war comics to *Robin Hood* to the *Hardy Boys*. Occasionally, I could identify with some small element in something I was reading—the friendship between Tom Sawyer
and Huck Finn, the fear and excitement of the all-male
world of *Treasure Island*, even *The Railway Children*, a sad
little book written at the turn of the century about some
children who endure poverty after their father has gone to
jail for embezzlement. I was ashamed of this last, because
I thought it had been written for girls; I tried to hide its
cover while I was reading it. Until high school, I read to
escape, to bring some color into what I unconsciously felt to
be a very boring young life.

Only when I began to encounter books intended for adults
did I realize that one could learn something concrete from
literature, that books could actually change your life, just
as the signs in the library said. *The Bridge of San Luis
Rey, Animal Farm, Catcher in the Rye*, then *Portrait of the
Artist as a Young Man*, then Henry James—I read what
everyone who eventually becomes a college English major
reads. But, at the same time, I was satisfying other aspects of
my literary curiosity more related to my budding libido.
Peyton Place, the first of the blockbuster sex novels, was
handed around surreptitiously when I was in the eighth
grade; I remember reading scenes over and over again,
excited and yet a little disgusted. I couldn't understand what
I was getting into; everybody wanted something in this book,
evidently the kind of thing priests warned me about in confession. These people felt really bad about it; they were

always getting in trouble and having to hide things. If I was going to grow up to live like that, I was afraid.

A few years later, *Lady Chatterley's Lover* burst forth in its unexpurgated version. I was beginning to understand that there were some books that were better than others, and I saw that this wasn't a "dirty" book. Lawrence's psychological expositions were new to me; his picture of Constance Chatterley was obviously meant to be the focus, but I realized that all of Lawrence's skill came out in describing Mellors, the gamekeeper. I was becoming aware of urges and questions that the book intensified but in no way satisfied. I wanted to know *why* Mellors wanted to have sex with this woman, and how he did it, and what he meant when he referred to his love for his commanding officer in the army. But Lawrence provided no easy answers. He was not concentrating on deep relations between men, and that is what I wanted to learn about. It was then, I think, that I began to realize that it would be very difficult to find out what I wanted to know. There was no one I could question about this, so I kept reading.

The summer between my junior and senior years in high school, I came across Thomas Mann's *The Magic Mountain* in a public library. No one had told me about it; I guess I chose it on the merits of reading its first few pages, my usual way of selecting books at that time. Here I finally encountered something to which I deeply responded. The infatuation that ten-year-old Hans Castorp felt for his schoolmate Pribislav Hippe corresponded to my first real infatuation. That I could identify so readily with little boys embarrassed me, yet I knew that I was reading something that was true and that I had never read anything that corresponded so closely to what I really felt. Castorp's later intense infatuation with the Russian woman was a magnificent description of the fixation common to all sexual directions that can become love. When I finally read *Death in Venice*, a few years later, I realized Mann provides one of the most serious and genuine approaches to complicated relationships of any novelist. He is not generally considered a "homosexual writer," but it is exactly his breadth of understanding applied to psychological and emotional interaction between men that must be considered an essential part of the literature on homosexuality.

I encountered another book during that last year of high school—*The Sergeant*, by Dennis Murphy. Although I didn't know it at the time, this book was an excellent example of the "serious" novels that dealt with homosexuality in the fifties and sixties. One of the main characters—a sergeant in the army—is a confirmed homosexual. The hero, a private under his command, gradually becomes aware of the sergeant's attraction to him. The younger man eventually becomes so disgusted with the sergeant that the latter gets himself killed, apparently out of remorse for inflicting his sickness on the younger man. Murphy wrote well; there was no reason, for me, an inexperienced reader, to think of this as other than a realistic portrayal of what I could expect if I ended up as a queer. I began thinking that I had better be careful, much more careful than the "normal" people around me appeared.

This impression was strongly confirmed when I eventually read *Giovanni's Room* by James Baldwin during my senior year in high school. In Baldwin's book—which assumed the status of a minor classic among homosexuals in the 1950's, according to people who read it when it originally appeared —a young American falls reluctantly into an affair with a young European. When he returns to his senses, the American leaves the European, who is pursued, trapped and tormented by a greasy older homosexual, whom he murders. The young European is speedily executed, and the hero begins to learn to live with his dreadful curse. There appeared to be an uncomfortable parallel between homosexuality and death in these books, and it frightened me. They were my only source of information outside of my own abortive experiments, and they held very little promise for any kind of future.

Eventually, I discovered the "classic" homosexual novels. Although very few had any semblance of literary worth, they filled a definite need. Foremost among them were such books as James Barr's *Quatrefoil* and Fritz Peters's *Finisterre*. In the latter, published in 1951, there are no overt descriptions of sex; rather, there are numerous languishing sighs, tender looks, and so on with some extremely provocative fade-outs at the end of chapters. The story, here mercifully condensed, tells of a wealthy young adolescent, who is in love with a tutor, who reciprocates his affection; the boy's evil stepfather, who evidently is lusting after him, makes some nasty intimations about the extent of the teacher-pupil relationship, and so gets the boy to confront his mother. She is highly upset and tells her son she would rather he were dead. He obliges her by drowning himself. The whole thing is absurd, written in the same silly but somehow touching style that distinguished Radclyffe Hall's *The Well of Loneliness*, a novel about lesbians that was banned in the 1920's. Typical of a whole generation of fiction, books like *Finisterre* were passed around secretly and pored over at great length; today, they have about as much relevance to young readers as have the *Hardy Boys*.

Gore Vidal has provided another classic of this genre, which even provides alternative endings that conveniently show the changes in social mores of which Vidal is so enamoured. *The City and the Pillar* somehow strayed onto a dorm room bookshelf when I was in college. Nobody seemed to have read it or even heard of it. I borrowed it for a few days and read it with a familiar feeling of unease. Vidal's story focuses on a single sexual experience that the hero, at fourteen, has with a close friend; this becomes the ideal by which he measures all later sexual encounters. He is consistently unhappy in all of these liaisons, so he is especially elated when he meets his old chum by chance. They have a few drinks and by some unlikely set of circumstances end up in the same hotel bed. The hero finally makes advances and is shocked when his friend disgustedly repulses him. In the first version, the book ended with the hero killing his friend; in the newer version, he merely rapes him. This was Vidal's first book, and one would be tempted to forgive its clumsiness if he had just let it lie in peace; unfortunately, he performed surgery on it only a short time before assaying *Myra Breckenridge*. A reader can only wonder why. (*Myra Breckenridge* isn't included in this list for several reasons. It has very little to do with its ostensible subjects, transsexualism and homosexuality; rather, it is a jumbled and occasionally funny guide to the whole world of American sexual confusion, appropriately using Hollywood as a backdrop and ultimate metaphor. Vidal, I think, is much more terrified of the breakdown of sex roles than most of his readers; in fact, this breakdown seems to be progressing quite calmly and successfully, with none of the barely restrained hysteria that his books so often exude.)

There are variations on this theme that end on a happier note. Sanford Friedman's *Totempole*, a novel that was not widely reviewed (and, sadly, is not very good) , confronts the problem of homosexuality head on. The problem consists of two issues: first, is the hero homosexual? This is obvious after the first few chapters to any but the most dull-witted readers. The second matter is perhaps trivial to the heterosexual reader who has strayed into the book; but it is often crucial in the lives of homosexuals. The question is simple: will the hero be able to perform anal intercourse, acting as the receptive partner? Luckily, he can, after a furtive little romance during the Korean war with a Japanese POW (who is an intellectual and a bisexual and therefore an acceptable partner in the eyes of the liberal straight reader).

There are also numerous descriptions of homosexuality in the best sellers that find their widest circulation as paperbacks. These books are usually programmed for some hypothetical straight, red-blooded American reader. Therefore, homosexual episodes are usually limited to interludes that show how far one can go in searching for the limits of depravity. In Harold Robbins's *The Carpetbaggers*, we are presented with a middle-aged film executive who is picked up by a rather sinister young man in a bar. We have been clued in that there is something wrong with the executive; it turns out that he is a repressed homosexual. When he returns with the young man to his house, the hustler presumes that the older man is a masochist and proceeds to beat him nearly senseless. The executive remains conscious enough to realize, however, that he enjoyed the sexual act (undescribed, like most of the couplings in Robbins's books) that was evidently performed in the course of his beatings; horrified at this realization, the executive castrates himself and dies. Thus homosexuality in Hollywood. To date, *The Carpetbaggers* has sold several million copies.

Another best seller, *Boys and Girls Together*, was written by William Goldman, who also wrote one of the classic sublimated-homosexual films, *Butch Cassidy and the Sundance Kid*. In his novel, Goldman describes the world of several people, including Aaron, a mother-fixated young man who is seduced by an older sergeant while he is in the army. Aaron eventually hits New York; his life there—portrayed rather well by Goldman, who lets most of his characters lead lives of stupefying boredom—consists primarily of pickups, particularly in movie theaters. Eventually Aaron is beaten nearly senseless by one of the pickups. This leads him to thoughts of a psychiatric cure, which are abandoned when he realizes it is "too late." Finally, Aaron meets an older man, an actor, who seems to desire a sort of idealized father-son relationship—something Aaron has been shown to want very badly. But, in an extremely cruel plot twist, the book ends with Aaron's being beaten—again, nearly senseless—by the actor—whom we discover to be an active sadist. This discovery takes place at the beginning of a long ocean voyage, a fitting symbol for the inescapable tortures that Aaron realizes he must face.

Another, more recent, example of the popular best seller that treats homosexuality that is not *really* homosexuality is James Kirkwood's *Good Times, Bad Times.* Hailed by reviewers as a top-rate thriller and a sensitive account of life in a boys' school, the book is little more than a crudely jazzed up *Catcher in the Rye.* What distinguishes it is the conflict between the friendship of two sensitive boys and the lust of their headmaster for the older of the two. A celebrated line, quoted by practically all of the reviewers, deals with the possibility of homosexuality in the relationship of the boys. "I mean, *anybody* would jerk off with Cary Grant if they got the chance." Since neither boy was Cary Grant, the relationship remains pure; they are both normal. Not so the headmaster, however. He torments both and finally, by his constant browbeating, causes one to die of a conveniently vague disease. The headmaster ends up stumbling through woods and swamps after the older boy, driven out of his mind by lust and jealousy. He catches the boy, fondles him, kisses him, and is killed by him for these unnatural acts. No one, of course, condones headmasters molesting their pupils. But it seems unfortunate that such a widely praised book shows homosexuality as the affliction of a crazed madman and the absence of it as crowning touch to a beautiful and pure friendship. Real-life situations where the exact opposite occurs in boys' lives will get little sympathy or understanding from liberal parents who read such "sensitive" books as

this obtuse and dull little story. Perhaps the simple acknowledgment of the existence of homosexuality in a mass-market
book sent the reviewers into such fits; one is even more
discouraged at the state of liberal thought on homosexuality,
if this is the case.

Something should probably be said here about a recent
best seller entitled *The Lord Won't Mind*. Accompanied by
a huge and successful barrage of publicity, this book quickly
sold over 50,000 copies in hard cover and went on to become
an enormously successful paperback. Hailed in its ads and
book jacket copy as "the most moving and outspoken novel
of homosexuality ever written," it is nothing more than soap
opera. The main characters are two distant cousins, Charlie
and Peter, who are both paragons of WASP beauty—blond
and spectacularly endowed. The plot revolves around the
struggle of the more delicate (read slightly smaller and
slightly less well-endowed) Peter to subdue the manly and
somewhat insensitive Charley so that he can call him darling
in public and keep house for him. Charley has an evil, pos-
sessive grandmother, who maliciously tells him that he has
Negro blood in him. When Peter finds this out, he says,
"Oh, darling, how marvelous. That must be why you smell
so funny." This remark is even more offensive in, than out
of context. Written by Gordon Merrick—who must have dug
up this manuscript from a trunk containing the results of
a late 1940's college creative writing course—the book is
ridiculous and harmful. The struggle for homosexuals to
determine their own lives does not deserve this racist, limited
parody of the ideal American couple. The fact that this book
did so well is perhaps testimony to the promotional genius
of its publishers, but it is even more indicative of the desperation with which homosexuals are seeking some realistic
picture of the way they might be able .to live. It is to the
discredit of Merrick and authors like him that they have
taken this need and preyed on it to create a market for pulp

romances that would never make *True Story* if they were about straight people.

Popular fiction is not, of course, an accurate representation of what may be considered current serious or enlightened thought on a controversial topic. But popular fiction does show directions of the "popular" attitudes that are often ignored by serious thinkers. And a pattern that is distinct and menacing begins to emerge in this popular fiction: Homosexuality, or any taint of it, is rewarded by death or abject humiliation. There are some exceptions, such as Friedman's novel or James Baldwin's *Another Country.* In the latter book, the main homosexual character falls into bed with the main heterosexual character after a night of heavy drinking; the heterosexual (who is, incidentally, the stablest male in the book) is gratified by his one homosexual experience with a friend but immediately realizes that it's not the life for him. Even though these books break the general rule that homosexuality leads to suffering and death, they still fail to show the homosexual as a complete being. Work, friendship, social and political consciousness, all are haphazardly sketched in, to provide a background for "the homosexual." There has been no major American author who has treated homosexuality in depth. Those writers who have dealt with it seem to have unconsciously adopted the classic attitude of homosexuality as either sin or neurosis. Thus, when they try to deal openly with love between persons of the same sex, they become so preoccupied with the matter of the character's homosexuality that they are unable to complete their creation of a genuinely complicated human being. "Homosexual" becomes a problem, rather than a natural part of the human condition.

There are a few classic books that treat relationships between males on more sophisticated levels. But most critics ignore or minimize the aspects of homosexuality in them. These books are unfortunately accessible only to readers acquainted with serious literature and criticism. Thus, the magnificent world of Proust, in which homosexuality is a crucial element, is given added richness by a reading of the vast body of criticism that explicates the mystery of Albertine, the hero's beloved, whom most critics believe to be a female disguise for one of Proust's male lovers, and the nether world of the well-bred homosexual in pre–World War I Paris. Likewise the novels and diaries of André Gide, which are so exciting and rewarding to anyone familiar with the development of modern French literature, would bore a young American reader who stumbled across them with no previous preparation. Hermann Hesse, whose immensely popular novels provide analyses of the relationships between men with many subtle insights, does not touch on the concrete physical expressions that have today come to be associated with such relationships. Of course one can learn about oneself through these books. But it takes a reader with more perseverance, intelligence, and intellectual honesty than most of us possess to make these books mean something concrete in his sexual life.

These books are certainly invaluable, but they are also irrelevant to the young reader who wants to understand his own feelings of homosexuality more clearly. There are a multitude of recent authors who treat homosexuality more explicitly, perhaps more exotically, and usually with much less skill. Jean Genet (whose special case I shall describe later), Jean Cocteau, Paul Bowles, James Purdy, Truman Capote, Ned Rorem—all take the reader's knowledge of homosexuality for granted. Moreover, their works incorporate subtle degrees of the social aversion to homosexuality, which they may be conscious of and even deplore but which is unconsciously transmitted to the reader. Thus, someone who strays into Alfred Chester's world of drug addicts and mother-fixated fantasizers or Rorem's circle of wits and eccentrics cannot be blamed for feeling confusion, trepidation, and even distaste for the homosexual world. Just as he might have reacted to the books of someone like Harold Robbins, he again wonders what could become of him in worlds like these, since he can find nothing that relates to his own life. Whatever the individual literary values of each book—whether they are ambitious, visionary, pretentious, serious, or precious, or all of these at once—they all share a sort of code that has been evolved to signal to the homosexual reader and to provide a defense against the contempt of the straight world.

The available sources of explicit information about physical sexual relationships are limited to pornography, which varies in quality. Medical and psychological books slight the actual performance of homosexual sex; there are scores of "how-to" sex manuals for heterosexuals, advising readers to throw restraint to the wind, but neither textbooks nor popular sex manuals even mention the possibility of homosexual intercourse. In the case of textbooks, this is probably because most such sources still seem to be oriented to the production of babies, despite the recent acceptance of birth control and legal abortions by the public. Sex manuals are meant to sell, with no complications; because homosexuality is socially unacceptable and descriptions of homosexual sex could keep a book from being widely distributed, the publishers prefer to leave such descriptions to pornography.

The first pornography I encountered was on the racks in the back of a seamy little drugstore in Washington, D.C. The magazines were primitive compared to what may be purchased today in such cities as New York, with its relaxing censorship laws. But, when I was in high school, these were dangerous, forbidden, exciting, and disturbing. The books consisted primarily of statuesque women and men in strained poses, wearing little or nothing, but with genitals invariably coyly hidden. I went to that store only four or five times over the course of my high school years, but the memory of the shame I felt each time has remained indelible. Why? I suppose I shared with most American children the feeling that sex was a secret and that bodies were to be hidden and concealed; that attitude was what caused such things as "dirty" pictures. But I was also more attracted to the pictures of men in the magazines, and I instinctively knew that was very wrong; they awakened something I had never before experienced. I have since realized that, although I knew even then these materials were pathetic, I was responding to something created expressly for me as a *homosexual*. This was my first glimpse of the world that has been created to service—and exploit—the homosexual. These magazines crudely showed men as nothing but sex objects; if they were objects, I could be one too. That frightened me then, and it infuriates me now.

With the relaxation of censorship enforcement in many cities, a wide selection of hard-core pornographic books has become available for every taste—sadistic, fetishistic, child-oriented, masochistic, voyeuristic, necrophilic, science fiction, frontier tales, and so on. Some have become immensely profitable. Richard Amory's series of *Loon* books are representative of this new wave of sexually explicit books in their detailed descriptions of sex between men. They are atypical, however, in the good humor and relaxed sensibility that makes them much less morbid than most pornography. With no pretense to literary quality, but with a genuine regard for homosexual desires and a real flair for characterization, Amory has created a fantasy world where no women intrude, where men are almost always able to relate deeply to one another, where no one has any lasting antagonisms. There are always a few villains, repressed homosexuals who are always brought out fairly early on. Despite the lack of realism and the unconscious male chauvinism, these books show people being affectionate to one another without fear, acting as people, not as bodies. One wonders why this positive attitude toward physical homosexuality has been primarily found in pornography until now.

There is a relatively new genre of homosexual pornography. Although it deals frankly with sex, the writing is usually highly stylized, and critics are hesitant to label such obviously sincere—and forcefully promoted—books as pornography. But there is very little in most of these books to distinguish them from run-of-the-mill skin books. Many of them seem to have been the lucky recipients of critical attention that needed a new and controversial topic. John Rechy's *City of Night* and *Numbers* are excellent examples of this school. His work portrays the milieu of the rootless young urban homosexuals who support themselves by commercial sex. Aspirations are not the same as achievement, however, and Rechy's work at best is a sort of tape-recorded true-life account of the lives of *some* homosexuals. The driven, compulsive young men that Rechy portrays do exist, and they do sacrifice their intelligence, their ambition, even their humanity in their search for an ultimate sexual experience that they know can never be attained. But Rechy's writing lacks the self-discipline that could make his characters more than two-dimensional shadows in his own private freak show.

The plight of Rechy as a writer is in many ways representative of the dilemma that faces anyone who attempts to depict homosexuality as something other than an ailment or a successfully handled liability. Rechy feels something that he desperately wants to express, but he has no cultural or aesthetic tradition other than the gossip of the homosexual subculture with which he can work. In *City of Night*, the only characters that are portrayed with much depth are the transvestites whom Rechy sees as caricatures of movie stars or glamour girls. But the macabre humor that Rechy allows these transvestites (who, incidentally, resemble no one I ever met in my somewhat limited contacts with cross-dressers) is absent from his next book, *Numbers*. The goal of the main character, Johnny Rio, is to have nonreciprocal sex with thirty men in the space of a week. When he nears his goal, however, he becomes terrified and reaches out for another young man who is as frightened as he. They fail to make any meaningful contact, and Johnny is once again on the prowl for numbers—men with whom one has sex—and now he is even more desperate and frightened. Rechy's characters are practically always desperate, frightened, on the run. His books are realistic, but they give no hint of the variety of homosexual life styles.

Hubert Selby's *Last Exit to Brooklyn* garnered even more critical acclaim, became a best seller, and was the center of several fierce censorship battles. But the tone of the book's reception showed how it followed in the death-and-damnation vein that runs through so much literature dealing with homosexuality. "A vision of hell so stern that it cannot be chuckled or raged aside."—*New York Times Book Review*. "A profound vision of hell. . . . An extraordinary book."—*San Francisco Examiner*. "No author that I can think of has presented so impressive . . . an account of the life of people at the bottom of the heap."—Granville Hicks, *Saturday Review*. The books consists of five stories about life in the heartlands of Brooklyn. Most of the characters are bitter and malicious, the remaining few simply stupid. Homosexuality, overt or latent, is the main theme of three of the stories. In the longest and best, a longshoreman who has become enamoured of a transvestite is rejected by her. His marriage maddens him, his work is boring, and he is extremely stupid, so he takes this rejection rather badly. So badly that he attempts fellatio on a ten-year-old boy. The boy calls the neighborhood punks, who slowly and in excruciating detail maim the man. This may be life at the bottom, but it is curiously unconnected to the real world. We feel nothing but disgust at the lives of these people. Any sympathy aroused is immediately superseded by relief that one's own life isn't *that* bad, at least.

Selby is an extremely idiosyncratic writer, using dialogue and narrative techniques reminiscent of socially conscious novelists of the 1930's. The world he describes, like that of Rechy's men, is unknown to practically everyone except those who have lived in it, and most of these have until now been uninterested in conveying the quality of their experience. Selby's work seems to have been strongly influenced by Jean Genet; but his depressing world view has none of the affirmation that Genet's characters so often have in their ferocious adversity. When Selby's characters display insight or initiative, it is usually born out of desperation. Selby's homosexual characters—the only ones who are portrayed with much depth—hover near insanity or are killed off. It is fascinating, and chilling, to realize, over and over again, the pattern of death and retribution that runs through American writing on homosexuality. The misery portrayed may exist, but it exists because homosexuality has traditionally been viewed as evil and degraded. The standard liberal response to books like Rechy's and Selby's merely affirms the scorn felt by the straight world for those "at the bottom of the heap." Rechy and Selby thus become the Stepin Fechits of the homosexual subculture: their books, however sincerely meant, reinforce the straight world's fear of the homosexual, and the straight world welcomes these books, calling them "profound," "extraordinary," and "impressive."

Jean Genet shares many characteristics with Selby and Rechy. He dwells on the violent and brutalizing aspects of homosexuality; he shows almost no reciprocal affection between men; he glorifies sexual gratification—in an almost religious manner. Yet Genet has become a worldwide celebrity, one of the few writers who is almost universally acknowledged as great. And he is one of history's most outspoken homosexuals. His autobiographical-fictional creations are exquisite blends of fantasy, gross realism, clinical sex descriptions, lyrical praises of bodies and faces, and sophisticated musings on the nature of reality, the possibilities of love and communication, and other issues central to modern thought. Genet has been analyzed and criticized from social, political, psychological, even sociological viewpoints. But the central fact of Genet's homosexuality is usually taken for granted, simply assumed as given by those who have no personal experience of it.

Genet's portrait of the homosexual underworld is often praised because it is the mirror image of the "normal" world. "The explication of the homosexual code becomes a satire on the heterosexual one. By virtue of their earnestness, Genet's community of pimps and fairies call into ridicule the behavior they so fervently imitate," writes Kate Millett. She shows how the degradation and contradictory hopes that Genet's characters experience are symbolic and expressive of the entire social order. Although she understands Genet much better than most of his other explicators, Millett cannot resist making Genet bear the burden of her particular and excruciatingly genuine oppression. "The political wisdom implicit in Genet's statement [in *The Balcony*] is that unless the ideology of real or fantasized virility is abandoned, unless the clinging to male supremacy as a birthright is finally foregone, all systems of oppression will continue to function simply by virtue of their logical and emotional mandate in the primary human situation. . . . Alone of our contemporary writers, Genet has taken thought of women as an oppressed group and revolutionary force, and chosen to identify with them. His own peculiar history, his analysis of expropriated peoples, inevitably lead Genet to empathize with what is scorned, relative, and subjugated."

But the "larger" ideas that Genet expresses are inseparable from the reality of the lives he writes about. Social roles, traditional concepts of masculine and feminine, the fury of oppressed peoples—all are portrayed by Genet, but they are portrayed in the lives of *homosexuals.* Readers may grasp and enthusiastically embrace these "larger" ideas, while still clinging to traditional concepts of homosexuality as something that is wrong.

Genet's style and content are as abstruse and demanding of careful study as those of Gide or Proust. The psychological processes that Genet describes are so complicated that they cannot legitimately be projected onto someone else's cause, to prove someone else's point; they must be accepted for what they are. Today being outrageous is good theater, good public relations, good business. Yet the public acceptance of Genet's outrageousness does not mean that his homosexuality can be viewed as anything but an aberration, to be equated with his criminal past. The patronization extended to Genet corresponds to that shown to women and black writers: a homosexual has been granted his say and has spoken at length, and the entire matter has been covered; the only people who could possibly be interested in hearing more would only be other homosexuals (or women or blacks). The "larger" issues that Genet illuminates are more important to the straight world, and it is ready to embrace them. But what straight readers and critics must remember is that homosexuality—the actual love of men for men—*is* the larger issue and is inseparable from everything else straight readers want to hear about. These readers must accept, understand, and even applaud Genet's homosexuality before they can begin to appreciate his work. I suspect that, if the present reading public really began to understand what Genet means, his popularity would diminish, at least until social and sexual attitudes change radically.

• • •

There *are* other views of homosexuality that counteract the essentially negative direction of most American literature on homosexuality. Interestingly, most of these are not American. Reasons for this are so varied and complex that it would be discursive to go into them here. But it is interesting to note that the often ridiculed American attitude of viewing foreigners as different, as somehow weaker, is still with us. Homosexuality is also equated with weakness, and so we must turn to the work of non-Americans to understand a phenomenon that is an integral, if largely ignored, part of American life. In a thought-provoking article in the *New American Review #1* (September, 1967), entitled "But He's a Homosexual . . . ," Benjamin De Mott considered the then current theory about a sort of informal conspiracy in the arts, fashion, and so on that was supposed to be threatening the fabric of American society. In refuting these patently absurd charges, De Mott also said a great deal about the real place of acknowledged homosexuals and homosexuality in literature and American life, mentioning such figures as Edward Albee, Tennessee Williams, and "their relevant superiors," such as Genet and Auden.

> With a few other poets and dramatists, they are the only compelling writers of the postwar period who seem to know anything beyond the level of cliché about human connectedness, whose minds break through the stereotypes of existential or Nietzschean extravagance into recognizable truths and intricacies of contemporary feeling. . . . A steady consciousness of a dark side of love that is neither homo- nor heterosexual but simply human pervades much of their work; they are in touch with facts of feeling that most men do not or cannot admit to thought. . . . They know that love and suffering are near allied, and that love ought not to be confused with the slumbrous affection or habitual exploitation that is the rule in numberless households.

Poets seem particularly able to deal with homosexual relationships in a realistic manner. W. H. Auden combines a literary sensibility of the highest order with a discreet, tender, yet thoroughly explicit exploration of homosexual love. Auden's poems rarely mention homosexuality openly; many that have nothing to do with homosexuality still include references, intonations, phrasings that are particularly accessible to homosexuals. His love poems are not addressed specifically to males, yet they are full of references to their direction—not hints or clues, for Auden is not trying to hide anything, but references that fit into Auden's entire poetic scheme. It is ironic that one of his most widely anthologized poems, "Lullaby," is usually ignored in this aspect. I wrote a paper on the poem in college. I spent an hour discussing it with a teacher, a man widely denounced on campus for being a "faggot," and the subject of homosexuality never came up. This whole side of Auden's work was ignored in every class in which I studied his work and every such class that I have heard of, and I cannot help but think that Auden's work is being crippled by this deliberate evasion. Oddly enough, *Life* magazine, the prayer book of middle America, made a discreet and unsensational note of Auden's homosexuality in an article on him in January, 1970. It was perhaps paranoid on my part, but I was offended by the article. To *Life* and its readers, Auden would automatically become an acceptable queer, a famous oddity who could be pictured at home in much the same way Edward R. Murrow used to corner celebrities at home. Auden's homosexuality should not be matter for revelation by *Life*; and yet it is.

Auden's sophisticated poems are, of course, simply not very interesting to many young homosexuals. Nor are the works of other poets likely to gain a wide acceptance. Thom Gunn, an English poet who has written extensively about homosexuality, is unknown among most gay as well as straight readers, despite his incisive work. There are numerous writers who portray homosexuality in constructive, realistic terms. One immediately thinks of Constantin Cavafy, the Egyptian-Greek poet who provided so many of the motifs for Lawrence Durrell's *Alexandrian Quartet*; or Yukio Mishima, the Japanese novelist and playwright whose tragic life encompassed a homosexuality that sought to return to primal simplicity in the middle of an industrial state; or even Edward Albee, whose supposedly "disguised" homosexual play *Who's Afraid of Virginia Woolf*, is a chilling, but believable, and meaningful study of people in crises. But, like those of Gide and Cocteau, the works of these writers remain mysteries to most readers. Even if they are known by reputation, these writers have their effect principally on literature and literary developments, rather than on people's lives.

I can only discuss books here that have worked for me, that have shown the way to functioning in a world I could understand. I came across the writings of Christopher Isherwood during a rainy Sunday afternoon in the library at college. I read straight through the *Berlin Stories* with their discreet (and therefore provocative) references to affairs with nameless persons, all in the shadow of Hitler's rise. I then read *A Single Man*, a relatively recent book, which tells of a middle-aged teacher's love for a younger man, who reciprocates. The younger man dies in an accident, and the older man mourns him and dies a few years later. A short book written in spare and unsentimental language, it depicts a mature relationship yet also provides a realistic look at the casual sex that is part of homosexuality. Never condemning or patronizing, Isherwood simply tells the story of a few people working out their problems. *A Single Man* could serve as an object lesson for many counselors, therapists, psychiatrists, and others who are incapable of realizing that there are aspects of homosexuality as completely normal and complex as anything encountered by heterosexuals.

Like Albee, Purdy, Vidal, and many others, Isherwood has made no outright statement about homosexuality. To accuse them of it could make me subject to a libel suit. So one must presume that their works are "fictions," that they are not speaking about their own experiences. A critic discussing such an author is forced to separate the author's life (unless he is dead) from his writings. It is simply another indication of the extent of homosexual oppression that an honest admission of homosexuality is not feasible for most of those who treat it in their work; it is—private, and somehow distasteful to broadcast that sort of thing. So the reader is left to learn what he can haphazardly, and writers must continue to behave as though they are not what they are writing about— even if they are. They may, of course, admit in private to certain sexual preferences, but the public must be protected from the obvious truth. It is as if most homosexual literature were a game, with elaborate rules, masks, costumes, hiding places. But the game is very old; we all know all the parts; the identity behind the masks is painfully clear. Everyone is tired of the old game, but there is no new one to take its place. And we are all unaccustomed to living without that game; it would be very painful to acknowledge that it all was a game, that there is nothing special going on anymore. It will probably hurt to live realistically, yet that is what we must do.

People like Isherwood can show the way to such realism. His book may not be great literature, but it is very good, very beautiful. If a literary work can be important and good for nonliterary reasons, his is. Another book in this mold is Marguerite Yourcenar's *Hadrian's Memoirs*, a highly complex novel in the form of a memoir of the Roman Emperor pointed out, in an ancient history class I attended several years ago, as a "good" ruler. I came across the book by chance in a secondhand bookshop and was surprised to learn that Hadrian was a homosexual. (These small shocks of recognition are numerous and often very funny; homosexuality is usually ignored in straight society, so one's personal list of famous homosexuals is a hodgepodge of famous, respectable, and surprising celebrities—all just as queer as you always felt you were.) The book is not a historical novel, in the lending-library sense; rather, it is a re-creation of what it was like to be an absolute ruler as well as a homosexual and how the emotional entanglements that all ordinary men feel became involved with politics.

There are very few modern novels that provide any *new* insights into homosexuality, but oddly enough, a few pornographic books point the way. Their graphic descriptions of sex-without-guilt are often accompanied by interesting writing on the place of *any* kind of sex in modern society. A typical example is *Hours*, by Lon Albert. One senses that it was written by a student in need of money—evidently a fairly common occurrence among pornography-writers. Set in the Columbia University community on New York's upper West Side, it concerns a radical, film-making, sexually innovative group of the kind that springs up around such campuses and details the interlocking lives of several people in this circle who come up against the Mafia. Despite the gratuitous sex, the book does give some very accurate descriptions of sexual types and habits among homosexuals—the men who touch and meet in the dark of theaters; the radical students who become less radical in the eyes of fellow activists when their homosexuality is made known; the well-adjusted young businessman who compulsively has anonymous sex and eventually is beaten; the belligerent, terrified, mother-centered alcoholic who finally goes into a "queer" sexual situation, where his only possible response is violence. Like many other commercial, sexually exploitative books being written today, *Hours* also represents an attempt to relate homosexuality to something other than hidden paranoid fantasies.

There are thus far relatively few serious nonfiction works

on the gay liberation movement. One of the most cogent and exciting is Carl Wittman's *Gay Manifesto*. Writing from his experience in San Francisco, Wittman discusses women, oppression, sexual roles, the gay ghetto, possible coalitions among oppressed groups and other topics in a reasonable, casual, and extremely appealing manner. Wittman is careful to avoid aligning himself with any of the various gay organizations that are proliferating throughout the country, although he does use militant language when stating his demands. His *Manifesto* is written in a personal style, but it is more than one person's opinion. He has distilled the countless hours of discussion and impassioned rhetoric that characterize militant homosexuality into a clear-cut list of grievances and demands. For anyone wishing to understand the goals of gay liberation, this is probably the best place to begin. The myriad statements, constitutions, and lists of goals that have erupted in the last few years contain few items that Wittman's *Manifesto* does not cover.

A few newspapers have begun to appear that present a personal approach to the meaning of gay liberation. They are completely different from the homosexual-oriented pulps that have been issued (with extremely profitable results) by publishers of such august sexist tabloids as *Screw*. The one with which I am best acquainted is *Come Out*, originally connected with New York's Gay Liberation Front and now speaking to and for New York's radical homosexual community. *Come Out* is published under severe financial and practical limitations. Due to its radical political-sexual politics, the paper must be printed at night, secretly; because the majority of people who work on it live outside the established economic order, they must devote time they would like to spend on the paper to eking out a living. Moreover, the paper's contents are decided by consensus; everyone involved in each article's appearance discusses and provides opinions on what is to be printed. The paper appears very irregularly; only six issues have been brought out since the paper's inception in the fall of 1969. But the resulting work shows a remarkable coherence of thought; it deals with every aspect of homosexuality but without the guilty prurience found in commercial papers. There are no sex ads, no suggestive pictures, no titillating fabrications of "personal experiences"—all of which characterize most sex publications, from such oddities as *Sexology* to the recent, supposedly amusing raunchiness of *Screw* and *Gay*.

Come Out is a serious venture; the problems discussed are real and painful ones, and the affirmations expressed are hard won and genuine. It is only through the development of media controlled by gay people that an accurate picture of the gay world can be presented. The straight press has seized on gay liberation as another item, a new fad to be played for jokes, now that the women's lib thing has gotten so serious. *Come Out* and the scores of papers like it—which are springing up all over the country and which are outside of the press establishment, the radical establishment, and the entire straight world—are now the sole recorders of the new homosexual consciousness.

The lack of meaningful literature on the positive aspects of homosexuality points to a painful necessity: the re-evaluation of all that has been written before and the extraordinarily difficult creation of a new kind of literature. The entire body of Western Judaeo-Christian literature has been created by individuals steeped in the sexism that characterized the growth of our culture. As we begin to outgrow the limitations of that culture and attempt to make a new one, we must recognize the problems inherent in appreciating traditional culture. This does not mean that we should abandon our heritage or deny the beauty and meaning of great works of art. We must learn, however, to be more critical of those values that are taken for granted. We are no longer in a family-oriented, expanding, colonizing culture. The virtues of that world, extolled for centuries, are meaningless to more and more people today. Likewise, many deeply rooted beliefs—for example, women are naturally weaker than men; homosexuality is unnatural; marriage is the standard and ultimately desirable state—must be discarded. These ideas, celebrated in innumerable and genuinely beautiful paintings, books, statues, films, were never "true." Rather, they were conveniences that helped a self-serving culture to grow. It *was* a healthy process, but it is not now.

The literature that will grow out of this new culture will reflect new values or, perhaps more accurately, a lack of the strict old values. And foremost among these will be the honest and accepting portrayal of people who relate to other people of their own sex. Ideally, this would be part of the sexual awakening that will enable everyone to break out of old stereotypes and achieve the freedom that has always been put forth as the ideal in every other area of human activity. But homosexuality, as the most despised, most denied sexual activity, must be treated with special care. The attempts by straight people and hostile homosexuals to understand the homosexual liberation movement are the most fitting form of reparation that can be made for the centuries of abuse, torture, and misery afflicted on those whose only crime was to feel affection for another man or woman. *Come Out,* the works of Auden, Isherwood, Hoffman, Wittman, all the writers and observers, past and present, who have written truly of homosexuals will be incorporated into this new culture and used as models for the new works. Above all, we must rid ourselves of the guilty, cruel, death-oriented fixations that dominate so much literature about homosexuals. Until we remove these one-sided representations of what homosexuals are *supposed* to be, we will never be able to develop fully.

I realize I have slighted many perhaps worthy books and

many passages in otherwise ordinary books that provide insights into homosexuality. But this was not meant to be a definitive survey of all homosexual literature; I leave that to sympathetic bibliographers and critics. Rather, this is a record of what one inquisitive person encountered, and the conclusions that he drew—was forced to draw—from what he read. It is a depressing picture for the most part, but it truly seems that the worst is over. There is no reason now why homosexuality cannot be portrayed as what it is—a full life.

4 meeting the GLF

In April, 1970, I decided to attend one of the dances sponsored by New York's Gay Liberation Front. I had been hesitant for several reasons. I had attempted to make New York's
bar scene quite a few times and, after each foray, had come
away determined to avoid gay bars in the future. The
atmosphere of the meat market, the desperation and inso-
lence of so many of the patrons, the sinister appearance of
the people who usually ran the places, the feeling of being
in a cage, a controlled environment, all made me extremely
wary of anything that resembled a gay bar.

In addition, I had heard something about the politics of
the GLF. It was supposed to be a radical organization that
functioned for homosexuals in somewhat the same manner

that Black Panthers did for blacks and the Young Lords for Puerto Ricans. I wondered how this representation, or whatever it was, worked. What, I asked myself, did politics have to do with one's personal sexual preferences? I had a great deal to learn.

At that time, the GLF held dances at Alternate University, a large loft that was the center for a free university, used primarily by New York's hip-radical community. Alternate U.'s activities ranged from karate classes to women's lib seminars to showings of films by radical film-makers. I knew all this by what I read in the *Village Voice* or what I had heard second- or third-hand. I had never been to the place before. I waited until about 10:30 to go to the dance, and I went alone, so I could leave easily if I didn't like it. Alternate U. was on the third floor of a large loft building; as I went up the stairs, I observed the people also going in. They were a very mixed bag—street people, straight-looking radical types, drag queens, college students. If they were homosexuals, most of them certainly didn't look it. That was a relief, at least.

At the door, there were several people collecting admissions. The charge was $1.50. I was surprised, since, if anything in New York becomes popular, prices are almost immediately raised as high as the market will bear and then raised again. (The Sanctuary, one of New York's poshest gay dance bars, charges $4 admission, which entitles you to one drink. Additional drinks are $1.50 apiece.) I paid and immediately headed for the bar; like many gay people, I tend to need a drink in strained or competitive social situations. There was beer and soda, at a quarter apiece. A *quarter* apiece? Something was funny here; the people who ran this place must be crazy. The rooms were packed; they could make a fortune, if they were smart. I got my beer and took up my station along the wall to check out the place.

It was hard to even get to the wall. Unlike most of the

bars I had been to, everyone here seemed to be moving. There was very little staring, although a lot of people were obviously very interested in a lot of other people. The music was loud, and many people were dancing, but this wasn't anything like the gay dance bars, where men danced with men in a heavily sexual atmosphere, with little shows and exhibitions being put on by individual characters. Here, men danced with men, women danced with women, and women and men danced together. People were dancing in groups also. There were all types of people, and many more who weren't types at all—all ages, black, white, Puerto Ricans, a few Orientals. And there were women, a lot of women. This was totally unexpected. I had not given much thought to the possible presence of women; I presumed they wouldn't be there. It was a dance for homosexuals, and I instinctively assumed that to mean men. I was fascinated by the lesbians, and a little frightened. I understood a lot about homosexual men, but these women were *really* queer; I understood nothing about them. (Later, I learned that many gay women felt the same way about homosexual men. This element of strangeness was a constant source of wonder; the fact that someone who, in the eyes of the rest of the world, shared our "perversion" was strange to us became a continual and salutary guard against the elitism that threatens any movement.) The most surprising thing about the dance was that all these people seemed to be having a good time. I had met very few people who admitted having a good time at a bar; the usual disclaimer was that bars were miserable but the only places to meet people in a relatively relaxed atmosphere.

I met several men that night. There were some who were familiar with the GLF and went out of their way to loosen up people who were nervous about the whole scene, as I evidently seemed to be. I was extremely wary of the all-encompassing warmth that accompanies so much in the hip community; it had always alienated me, because it seemed to relegate everyone to the status of being on "our" side. There was the same feeling here to a certain extent; everyone was almost professionally friendly, almost ostentatiously tolerant. But I also eventually realized that something else was going on. The cheerfulness had another quality, that of a people caught together in some disaster. There was a feeling of "us" and "them," and rightly so, for everybody in the room was gay, and they had come together to affirm themselves as gay. There was a sort of justified paranoia; the straight world may not like it, many other gay people may not like it, but these people were not hiding anything.

These thoughts came later; that night was a series of sensations and impressions that were challenging, confusing, and, above all, intense. I had crossed a line, quickly but irrevocably. Earlier, I had left my apartment after dinner with some straight friends. They knew that I was not involved in their scene of dating, of finding a girl to live with, of marriage; I had lived alone, and worked hard, and went out a lot. My job with a publishing firm kept me abreast of current trends in radical politics; it also gave me the professional's jaundiced eye, the detachment that comes from working with and handling ideas rather than formulating and believing in them. But, when I went to that dance, I had left my detachment behind. I danced with men. I talked openly about sex between men. I relaxed in a social situation, instead of wondering how I should or could relate to women, as I did in most straight gatherings with people I didn't know. Instead of competing or coldly evaluating, as I did in most homosexual gathering places, I relaxed. I looked around, talked to whomever I wanted, let people approach me without worrying about whether I was being cool enough.

Although I had read a little about the Gay Liberation Front, the dance was my first contact with the group, and it characterized the entire direction of the GLF—exciting, chaotic, undisciplined, flamboyant, and powerful. I met many people that night, including a young writer on his way to Europe from San Francisco, the city that was supposed to be a homosexual mecca. He was amazed at the relaxation and freedom exhibited at the dance. When I asked him why, he told me that, in San Francisco, men are not allowed to dance together during slow dances, but may during fast songs. I later learned that the same rules were enforced until recently in Chicago.

I also met a quiet, frail-looking, and extremely funny young man who turned out to be a hairdresser. He was exactly what the straight world expects homosexuals to look like—long, blond, beautifully cut hair, fine features, expensive clothes, a delicate, almost "effeminate" air about him. He was also extremely articulate and, I soon found out, fiercely hostile to the straight world that surrounded him and too often attempted to characterize him. Like many people in the Gay Liberation Front, he had been politically inactive before encountering it. He told me he had been attending meetings and dances for a few months, and, only in the last few weeks, had he come to agree with much of what the GLF stood for. At one point, he said, "I don't *have* to take any more shit."

I noticed a lot of street people at the dance, and the ones I talked to revealed to me a whole new segment of the homosexual world. They were "long hairs," who would be taken as standard hippies by the straight world. But they were active, practicing homosexuals, and as such they were often antagonized by the straight hip-radical community. These street people were the most articulate and active figures in the Gay Liberation Front—perhaps, I later thought, because they had very little to lose. But they frightened me a bit, these strange people who were a double threat to the middle class from which I came. Not only did they abjure 9-to-5 living, churches, formal higher education, marriage, upward mobility, the *New Yorker,* and every other middle-class convention, but also they violated all sexual mores—and, in this, they went far, far beyond the weekend hippies and conventional hip people. They did whatever they wanted to in bed with whomever they wanted, and they aggressively proclaimed their right to do so. They were a far cry from the stereotyped pansies and dykes, and yet they welcomed and acknowledged those who still represented these stereotypes. The mingling of all these people in one room was a puzzling, exhilarating, and encouraging sight.

I left the dance tired, extremely curious, and alone. I had felt under no compulsion to pick someone up, to score, as I probably would have in the atmosphere of most gay bars. I didn't know why the whole scene was less competitive, but it was, and that was a relief. I felt somehow as if a very heavy burden had been lifted from my shoulders—one I had never noticed before and was only now beginning to understand.

• • •

I had seen the little two-line ads that the Gay Liberation Front ran in the *Village Voice* about its meetings, and so I decided to attend one at the next available opportunity, which turned out to be the following Sunday. When I first attended meetings, the GLF met at the Church of the Holy Apostles, in the Chelsea section of New York, bordering on Greenwich Village. One approaches the church through a maze of high-rise middle-income apartments. Nestled in among them, the church is comfortably anachronistic—ivy-covered, with stained-glass windows and a few old trees sheltering the adjoining parish house.

Like most newcomers, I was extremely nervous at that first meeting. I had literally no idea of what to expect. The gathering was typical of most of the others I attended. When I entered, there were about forty to fifty people in the room, about two men to each woman. They represented about the same mixture I had seen at the dance, but now they were all sitting quietly in a large oval, listening to a speaker who was evidently some sort of chairman.

I remember that my palms were sweating; that tension now seems almost laughable, but I have realized that it did exist, primarily because, for the first time, I was making a public declaration of my personal sexuality outside a safe, all-male—and highly competitive—sexual marketplace. I felt the familiar tensions: did I look all right? was I saying the right things? or keeping silent at the right times? This self-absorption rapidly evaporated as I realized no one was evaluating me. In fact, very few people were doing anything but listening to the speaker.

There were several heated discussions that evening, most of which bewildered me. They were evidently ongoing discussions, and nobody could spare the time in the rapid-fire dialogues to fill in newcomers. But the talk was thoroughly engrossing, and, throughout the evening, I was repeatedly amazed at the frankness and lack of posing of most of the speakers.

I soon found that the GLF meetings were also unique in their procedure. The entire group decided on issues and projects by consensus; the standard minidemocracy that most organizations used to vote and move on to other matters was not feasible for the GLF. When these women and men put the most intimate aspects of their lives on the line, they felt it imperative that the fullest possible agreement be reached on all decisions. If votes were used, blocs would be formed, deals would be made, and the group would eventually face compromise rather than confrontation. Chairmen were chosen by lot. After serving for four meetings, the chairman was re-placed and a new chairman of the opposite sex chosen, again by lot. The people moderated the discussions, which often went on for hours, and every issue was agreed upon by all present.

Many times, there were objections raised to this procedure, particularly by new people. They could not see why so much time was wasted, a problem I soon noticed, but I saw no other way out than that chosen by the GLF. There was another problem in that new people showed up at each meeting, sounded off, and then disappeared. Some people who had been attending regularly would protest at the newcomers and their ideas; they felt, understandably, that these new people were interlopers. But such frictions and disagreements periodically disappeared when a newcomer would shyly preface a question with some explanation like "This is my first meeting, I'm not really a member yet . . . ," which would be followed immediately by a spontaneous shout from everyone present—"We are all members!"

This openness is what has continued to impress me most deeply about the Gay Liberation Front, despite reservations that later developed. There was finally a place that one could go to freely, where one could keep to oneself or immediately get involved, where one did not have to commit oneself to being a "member" in order to feel that he belonged. There were never dues. There were no rules of order except that one be recognized by the chairman. There was no one taking minutes or counting heads. The only absolute was confrontation. Everyone in the GLF confronted the entire straight world, and often one another as well.

The Gay Liberation Front had been formed almost a year earlier, in July, 1969, about a month after the first Christopher Street riots. The founders had been an extremely diverse group, from a variety of backgrounds. After the riots, these people had gone to the Mattachine Society, a long-established homophile group that had until recently been the leading spokesman for the homosexual community. An Action Committee of the Mattachine Society was formed, which immediately started handing out flyers explaining the riots and calling gay people to unite and protest the oppression of homosexuals, as well as the recent events at the Stonewall Inn. The Mattachine Society, never noted for its radical politics, became extremely alarmed at the militant stance of its new members, as well as their radical political thought on matters not pertaining specifically to homosexuality. Finally Mattachine's president suggested that the Gay Liberation Front— the name had been spontaneously adopted after being suggested by one of the founders—find a new home as soon as possible. The GLF women and men then joined with a group of radical homosexuals who had been meeting informally at Alternate U., and they all decided to keep the name. After several months of meeting at the Washington Square Methodist Church and Alternate U., meetings were switched to the Church of the Holy Apostles in January, 1970. (A significant phenomenon is the continuing receptivity of churches to homosexual activists who need facilities. Although many homosexuals are violently prejudiced—and justifiably so—against the religions that have condemned them for so many centuries, the churches and their pastors seem determined to make amends for past sins by welcoming the homosexual community at every opportunity. In addition to the two churches mentioned above, which are regularly used for homosexual meetings and symposiums, there are weekly dances at Saint Peter's, an Episcopal church, as well as the countless forums and discussions groups sponsored by churches throughout the country.)

The GLF is the least structured large group I have ever been involved with. Every meeting ranged over such a variety of topics that a sampling of them can only approximate the often surreal quality of these gatherings. The Black Panthers were a constant source of confusion and consternation. Support for the Panthers at a Bastille Day rally became a crucial factor in the original split of the GLF from the Mattachine Society. When I first started attending meetings, there was a great deal of impassioned discussion over how far the GLF should go in supporting the Panthers. Black groups persisted in calling white policemen and politicians "faggots"; Eldridge Cleaver never clarified his statement that "homosexuality is a sickness, just as are baby-rape or wanting to become the head of General Motors." Because the majority in the GLF supported most aims of the Panthers, there was widespread disappointment and disillusion when the Panthers initially refused to consider even the possibility of opening a dialogue with the GLF. Heated debates about contributing money to the Panthers' bail fund repeatedly were interrupted by outbursts condemning the Panthers' sexism. The situation was finally eased when Huey P. Newton called for the recognition of the oppression of women and gay people as well as blacks.

The only Black Panthers I had ever seen had been on television. Like most liberals, I was at once fascinated and frightened by their demands. They had always seemed somehow . . . foreign. But now I, as a homosexual, was involved in a serious, equally matched confrontation with them. I had always thought of the black-white struggle as the most crucial problem of the many facing America. But I was also beginning to realize that there was a deeply rooted problem involving sexism, sexual stereotypes and role-playing, and it was a problem I was intimately affected by. The Panthers were rightfully suspicious of being co-opted by white liberals, and I was beginning to understand that suspicion. I could never really understand what it means to be black; I may sympathize and empathize, but I will never *know*. Likewise, a black man will never understand my oppression unless he is a homosexual; indeed, there is no reason why he should. We are all in this struggle together, and yet our oppressions are different, and so we must continue to confront each other. I gradually reached these conclusions, after listening to hours of debate; I never did see a Black Panther, but I came to understand what I had to fight for and even began to perceive dimly what the blacks had to fight for. I would never be able to presume glibly, however, that I understood how any other minority group felt.

More immediate and pressing problems developed almost immediately. The GLF, like most radical groups, was the scene of constant power struggles and factional infighting. I felt deeply about things the GLF revealed to me—the extent of my oppression, the distance from the straight world that I had always felt and never admitted, the need for an immediate change. But I also felt a great distance between myself and the majority of the women and men in the GLF. I was a child of the aspiring middle class, and I had worked too hard for my education, my clothes, my furniture, all the trappings of straight bourgeois society, to be able to cast them back over my shoulder without a thought. Moreover, I felt a genuine sense of responsibility to my family, a responsibility that most people in GLF could not understand and many condemned. I could not devote *all* my time and energy to the movement, and I was put off when I was at times regarded with the paranoia that faces all newcomers to radical groups. Most of all, I was afraid of the internal politics. There were not supposed to be leaders, but there were. There was supposed to be consensus, but often there was not. I agreed with GLF goals and statements, but I did not know how I could help to achieve them by doing anything except attending meetings.

At one of my first meetings I heard a reference to a consciousness-raising group. I didn't know what that was, although I had heard the term used in reference to women's liberation. I soon found out that this was the best way for me, personally, to work toward some sort of homosexual liberation. Like the communist cell concept, consciousness-raising groups are designed to make each member committed to beliefs that they constantly discuss, hammer out, and revise. Once I discovered these small groups, I was never again as able to respond to the mass-followers aspects of the Gay Liberation Front or any other homophile group.

• • •

The regular Sunday night GLF meetings were, and are, classic studies in chaos. The fierce competition for attention that is characteristic of the homosexual social milieu was channeled into more constructive but exhausting struggles to deal with the vast number of problems. The range of these problems was inspiring, but it also put me off. I wanted to do something, to learn something that was going to make me part of the movement. Yet I *couldn't* devote my whole life to gay liberation. I couldn't worry equally about the oppression of the Panthers in relation to the oppression of homosexuals, the oppression of gay women by gay men, the need for day care centers, the solidarity demonstrations that were often called to support homosexuals who were being harassed by the police, the need for understanding the (to me) rather frightening transvestites who were beginning to take an active part in gay liberation. So, when I heard someone announce at a meeting that new consciousness-raising groups were being formed, I welcomed the chance to participate in something more personally involving. After the meeting that Sunday night, several people agreed to meet at one man's apartment the next Wednesday night.

There were only three people who showed up that night to form the new group; we were disappointed, but I, at least, was also secretly relieved that there was not a large crowd of people to argue, propose plans and projects, and disperse in confusion. Two young men who were veterans of other consciousness-raising groups also arrived to help us achieve some sort of direction in our first few sessions. The three of us that night were typical of those who eventually formed the final group—a middle-level office worker in a brokerage house, a radical activist who had only recently come out, and me, a publisher's copy writer making vague attempts to drop out. There were thirteen people the next week, and the group eventually leveled off at about eight, but the tensions and constructive possibilities inherent in these diverse life styles continued to characterize our meetings.

The recent interest in therapy groups, encounter groups, and sensitivity training has reached the proportions of a fad. But the underlying needs that these often pointless exercises meet are serious, and these groups, as foolish and even dangerous as they sometimes are, remain viable ways of confronting those problems—loneliness, anomie, powerlessness in the face of institutions and ideologies, the lack of meaningful work. Despite the good and legitimate reasons for unhappiness that caused people to seek out these groups, I had never personally felt comfortable about participating. The idea of instant intimacy depressed me, and the probability that any insights gained with a group of strangers would become invalid outside that context made me disregard the entire phenomenon of encounter groups. The consciousness-raising technique, however, seemed much more promising; what I learned about it at that first meeting confirmed my initial optimism.

Looking back, I realize that one of the factors most responsible for my being able to function in this group situation in contrast to other groups, which usually made me extremely wary, was that we were all homosexuals. I had always instinctively drawn a self-protective circle around myself when I was involved in intellectual group activities. I had said to myself, "This is an interesting situation, but you must watch your step. These people shouldn't have to contend with your personal problems. Besides, your homosexuality isn't *that* important, anyway. Nobody really cares. So, to avoid any unpleasantness, just watch your step." And I did. I listened to straight friends and acquaintances talk about their emotional relationships, feelings, fears; I listened carefully and gave what I hoped was sincere, good advice. I never talked about any of my personal problems in any terms but the most abstract; for example, I would say, "If a person likes someone. . . ." No names or sexes were mentioned. It wasn't worth boring or offending my friends. In short, I took the petty problems of the straight world more seriously than I did my own immediate concerns about my homosexuality. It took several years for me to realize how boring, let alone wasteful, such a hypocritical process could be.

Now I was finally able to talk with people realistically. We were strangers, and we were not initially interested sexually in one another. We had met to discuss the problems surrounding our lives as homosexuals. This was not a simple rap session, like those endless hours of gossip in bars, restaurants, living rooms that fill the lives of New Yorkers, straight and gay. We had specific goals and, as I quickly discovered, a specific format. The two men who were experienced in consciousness-raising described the standard session, and that is the format we followed until our group dissolved, about five months later.

Members of the group meet once a week, or more often, if they can manage it, at the homes of individual members. The meeting places are switched as often as possible; this turned out to be fairly important, because many people (including myself) were not used to being with groups of homosexuals at home. Each week a topic was offered, and, if anyone couldn't or wouldn't talk about that topic, another was chosen. Each person spoke about his experiences, with as few interruptions for clarification as possible. One member took notes and, after everyone had spoken, the whole group talked about what had been said and attempted to discover some patterns and draw some conclusions. The procedure may seem perhaps mechanical and even sterile, but, in practice, the evenings were sometimes strange and sometimes frightening, often exhilarating, occasionally stupefyingly dull, but always engrossing.

One of the main questions was: what are we aiming at in this group? We never did settle the issues satisfactorily, nor has anyone in any other group I have talked with. But we came up with some directions that could serve as a fair approximation of what consciousness-raising is about. Each of these groups was attempting to help each member realize the extent of his oppression as a homosexual, how that oppression was forced on him as a child, how his society helped it to develop, and finally what could be done to break these patterns of oppression and create a more realistic and freer life, one that acknowledges and enjoys homosexuality rather than hiding it. It is difficult to explain how quickly and painfully these rather abstract concepts—oppression, role-playing, our restrictive society, and so on—became immediate concerns.

In those first few sessions, we were constantly amazed—at the many incredible similarities in our development, at the seemingly incomprehensible choices that some of us had made, but most of all at the realization that we had indeed stumbled on something important, that the nameless anxiety, self-consciousness, and petulance that had plagued us for years were the signs of our oppression. There was no attempt, as one might imagine, to absolve ourselves of responsibility for our lives; rather, there was a sort of unspoken, surprised guilt that we had allowed ourselves to be driven so far from what we wanted and needed.

Perhaps the best way to illustrate these developments is to describe some of the topics we agreed upon. The first one was "coming out." "Coming out," for the uninitiated, is the gay term for an individual's first active expression of his

homosexuality. Each of us told, in vivid detail, what his
family background was, how he had felt himself attracted to
men, when and where his first homosexual experience had
taken place. What was most surprising was the diversity of
background; there was no pattern of domineering mothers or
competitive fathers or weakening traditional values to account for our homosexuality. Our backgrounds were as varied
and complex as those in any straight group. Despite all the
talk about the possible causes of homosexuality that I had
read about, there seemed to be no more discernible *cause* for
homosexuality in this group than there was any *cause* for
heterosexuality in any random group of straights.

But there were other, definite patterns. All spoke about the
guilt that they eventually felt. There were men from Irish
blue-collar backgrounds, progressive Jewish professional
families, suburbs that had sprung up all over postwar America, farms in the Midwest and the deep South. Some of us
had come out early, some had come out only when they left
college, but we all shared a fear of rejection by those near us,
no matter how radical or tolerant. This fear of exposure and
the fear of revulsion by family and friends had been left behind by only a few of us. We agreed totally on very few
things, but on this issue we never faltered: We had come
together to throw off our guilt, and this intent underlay all
our actions.

There were more parallels. We were all antireligious to
some extent—not an uncommon phenomenon among young
people in New York, but significant in light of all organized
religions' past condemnation of homosexuality and their recent liberalized attitudes. We were also all college-educated—
some were dropouts, but all of us had attended some institution of higher learning. And we were all, despite differences
in our ages, very sexually experienced. This turned out to be
an important consideration, because we could remember and
present examples from our own lives, rather than theorize

about abstractions—a very common fault among those who discuss homosexuality without having experienced it.

One topic that provided some surprising insights was the existence—or lack of it—of sexual preferences for one type of person over another. At first, the group broke down roughly into two factions—those who acknowledged and enjoyed preferring certain types of people and those who denied any such rigid standards of selection. What surprised us, however, as we reviewed what we had said, was that we all concentrated on types of people rather than individuals. We were responding in most cases to types or images of what we were conditioned to expect. Some people were fairly simple in their demands—tall, slender blondes, dark men with mustaches. Others were more subtle in their preferences, and less conscious of their patterns. The most "radical" member, for example, found that he would instinctively consider third-world, radical, and activist men somehow more interesting and somehow more "real" than the middle-class men who formed the great body of self-acknowledged homosexuals. Yet he had serious involvements only with men of his own social background—well-educated, extremely literate, and usually as straight-appearing as he was.

I had always prided myself about the painful insights I had already gained into my own homosexual experience. I quickly realized, however, that there was a lot I was going to have to relearn. On the matter of types, for example, I had assumed that there were no biases in my choices: everybody had preferences, it was only natural, but it didn't *mean* anything. I found out that the only people I considered as anything other than sex objects, anonymous people to be used, were men who were a lot like myself, but who, I thought, possessed ideal versions of whatever qualities I felt I lacked. The concept of using people as objects was a standard GLF criticism of homosexuals' oppression of themselves. I readily agreed that this was what I and many others did, but it took months for me to realize what I was saying and attempt to change.

Consciousness-raising groups can develop into several forms, or they can dissolve. The group that I participated in eventually dissolved, as soon as its possibilities for growth and learning were exhausted. We had all heard stories about people in other groups becoming fast friends, meeting for dinner several times a week, even eventually working together at some full-time project. We were all disappointed when this did not happen to us; in the first burst of understanding each other, we had hoped that something permanent would develop to sustain the feeling of unity. As members moved away or became more involved in their other work or developed new and time-consuming relationships, we each realized that the insights we had gained had induced a sort of euphoria that was dangerous to our total development. The simple realization that there was nothing wrong with homosexuality was not enough; the process had to be continually expanding to be meaningful. Once we found out what we were, we had to decide what we could become.

There were some evenings in those few months that remain vivid in my memory. One night, shortly after we had started meeting, about a dozen people were gathered in a small apartment in the East Village. It was very hot, and we were all bored. The group was still shaking down to its eventual membership of eight, and we weren't used to talking openly in front of each other. The topic that night was what we liked or disliked about homosexuals as a group or class. I was busy with my own little interior monologue—arguing fine points of behavior, ignoring too much of the proceedings, and attempting to figure out how best to express myself during my turn. When it finally did arrive, I was dumfounded for a moment; the adviser from another group who was still helping us waited and then prompted me to go on. I started talking, and a lot of things poured out that I had never meant to say. I talked about my fears of certain kinds of effeminate homosexuals and my intense dislike for the leather-clad pseudo-motorcyclists who were the exact opposite. I kept going, talking about my inability to function well in the deperson-alized vacuum that characterizes most New York life. Finally, I came to what was bothering me most—the patronizing, mechanical acceptance by hip people, gay and straight, of what was supposed to be "real" and sincere, the goal of being together that denied any display of need or weakness and yet condemned obvious strengths. I was embarrassed, unable to meet anyone else's eyes, and yet I wanted to finish what I had to say. I had never formulated these thoughts. They were spontaneous expressions of what was bothering me, and they probably would not have been expressed for years—if ever—if I hadn't been able to talk with these people.

Everyone kept quiet until I was finished, and then they discussed what I had said and questioned what they did not understand. They understood the intensity of what I had said, and yet they did not let me off with any false feelings of consideration. We were still strangers, and they could be impartial like strangers. The whole episode was a sort of catharsis, and yet it had none of the melodramatic overtones associated with the emotional explosions of encounter groups. This was essentially an intellectual awakening; I was cer-tainly involved emotionally, but I was noting at the same time, with amazement, observations, prejudices, biases, in-sights I had never realized were in my head. That night was the first time I felt a real tie developing with the group; it stood me in good stead later.

The same kind of immediacy was felt a few weeks later, on another hot night, in another cramped Village apartment. That night we were discussing sexual types and preferences. The mood was again lethargic, although everyone was inter-ested in the discussion. A comfortable aura of gossip hovered around such topics, making it much easier to talk freely about our personal lives. A small, dark-haired young man of about twenty began to speak; he apologized for being incoherent, he said, but he had worked a double shift that day after being stoned. Suddenly, he started talking faster. He said that he was unhappy with his life. He was tired of the standard homosexual promiscuity. He was tired of cruising and being cruised. He was tired, most of all, of being lonely. He went on, in specific, anguishing detail, and the rest of us sat there open-mouthed. He was a nice-looking, rather boyish man, and we had assumed that he was as cheerful as he had seemed to be—a nice cheerful boy. We were shocked at the depth of his feeling and bitterness; we were even more surprised at the extent to which he expressed our own unacknowledged feelings. The group was beginning to work, and it was a lot more serious than we had anticipated.

The group functioned from the beginning of May, 1970, until about the middle of September. According to anyone's standards but our own, the group may not have been particularly successful. Each of us emphasized, however, at the last few meetings, that, even though we knew the group was dissolving, we *had* accomplished something really meaningful. Each of us had started reconciling the relation of our personal homosexuality with our work, whatever it might be. The necessity of hiding homosexuality from straight co-workers was an incredible and unnecessary burden to many of us. Even if we had to continue the charade, for practical purposes, we realized that the artificial but incredibly rigid boundary between "life" and "job" was even more deadening for homosexuals than for other bored American malcontents.

We had also realized where each of us stood in relation to the gay liberation movement and the whole radical left. Most of us were not completely into the gay lib life style of constant meetings, constant confrontation with every aspect of the straight world, and communal living. We subscribed to a lot of the movement's aims without subscribing to them all personally; this was a real problem for the few people who were extremely active in gay lib, but we quickly realized that these differences could not be resolved in the group meetings, if indeed they should be. Moreover, we felt that the variety of approaches to homosexual life styles was invigorating; we all had something other with which to contrast our own experiences.

There were other, more prosaic, useful results. As one man put it after a rather emotional exchange on the relative merits of cruising bars for sexual partners or simply meeting people in the course of one's everyday activities, "Sometimes I wonder if we're trying to learn anything more here than how we can make out better." Everyone protested that our motives were nobler, but we all acknowledged that we really were also trying to figure out how to make out better, how to be happier with other people. And the group discussions did help us in many small ways. We pointed out annoying traits in each other's conversations and discussed attitudes toward women and other homosexuals in situations outside the group, humor related to sex, even clothing. I remember one man who always removed his shirt during particularly hot meetings. We all noticed, but, for several weeks, no one commented on it. Finally, one person mentioned how, at a mixed gay dance, a lot of men quickly removed their shirts because of the heat, but that women never did, and how that social sanction, even in a radical, sexually permissive atmosphere, must bother the women. We then confronted the man in our group who, we all had felt, individually, was displaying himself as a sexual object. He was unconscious of the attitude and became defensive; we were surprised and a little ashamed that we had each been too embarrassed to bring up such a small but definitely annoying matter in the group for fear of appearing foolish to the others. This kind of small but meaningful confrontation taught us all a great deal about our subtle, unconscious, or merely self-conscious attitudes about each other and about homosexuality.

Finally, the group taught us how to let go of each other.

The homosexual subculture that has been patronizingly described in numerous articles and studies is always pictured
as an exaggerated and pathetic version of an all-female society. The caricatures of *The Boys in the Band* pointed up this
aspect of homosexuality. Much of the action portrayed could
have happened in the homes of thousands of New York
homosexuals, but it was in no way a portrait of all homosexuals or representative of homosexuality as a life style. But
certain social elements *have* become typical of the various
homosexual scenes: a high degree of loneliness, a sometimes
near compulsive need for sexual activity to prove that one
can relate to the outside world, a careful distinction between
one's friends and one's sex partners. These attitudes may be
self-imposed, but they are also the result of centuries of oppressive social forces. The undeniable loneliness and confusion that each of us in the group had felt as homosexuals
was greatly eased by participating in these open exchanges.
And so strong became the feeling of unity that for a while
we all thought that there might be a sort of insoluble bond
uniting us. Eventually we found that, although we liked and
admired each other, we did not have to become lifelong
friends. Even if several people in the group related sexually
with others at various times, there was no need for a crisis to
develop if these relationships did not continue. Our lives as
homosexuals were not so desperate that we had to cling to
each other like drowning men. We could learn from each
other, and move on, and come back to each other. And so
we did.

Several of the people in my group left New York for vary-
ing lengths of time, one permanently. I became involved in
another group, which met sporadically for a couple of
months, but I quickly realized that it held very little future
for me. There are no statistics on the success or life expec-
tancy of groups, and I hope there never will be. I know that at
least as many never get off the ground as make it and that

very few really effect significant changes in the participants' lives. But they are perhaps the best possible way to relate personally to homosexual liberation. I eventually participated in another group, one that went much further in affecting my personal life.

• • •

The most visible affirmation of my involvement in the gay liberation movement came on June 28, 1970, when I took part in the first annual Christopher Street Liberation Day parade. This was the first anniversary of the riots that had erupted when police raided the Village's most popular gay dance bar, the Stonewall. These riots had led to the founding of the Gay Liberation Front, the Gay Activists' Alliance, and eventually to the numerous groups that are now proliferating all over New York. The celebration of that revolt was the occasion for marches in New York, Los Angeles, and other large cities; in New York, there were also numerous workshops, seminars, film showings, crash pads, and open houses. Gay liberation had come a long way.

But on the night of June 28, 1969, there had been no thought of organizations or fronts or movements, but only a spontaneous rage at what seemed to be cruel and unnecessary harassment. The police evidently thought of it as a standard raid on a gay bar: they would go in, get everybody out, arrest a few people, and close the place down until the violations were rectified or the payoff was made. But that night something snapped. No one wanted to be pushed around, and all the queers started pushing back. No one submitted willingly to arrest, and soon the police were barricaded inside the bar, trapped by a hail of bottles and stones thrown by the angry crowd outside. The police were eventually rescued by more police, and there were several arrests; as in most cases involving homosexual disturbances, exactly which people were arrested, what they were charged with, and what eventually happened to them is hard to find out. There were disturbances for several nights after that, with curiosity-seekers coming to gawk at the strange confrontation between police, angry street homosexuals, and the straight "liberal" residents of the area who could not understand what these nice, funny little faggots were so upset about.

I got in late the night of the riots; it was a Saturday, and I had been to a film and gone drinking with some straight friends. An announcer broke into the music on a hip FM radio station and, in a puzzled voice, gave some sketchy description of what was going on in the Village. I remember being curiously elated. I wanted to call up my straight friends and tell them about it, but I quickly decided that they wouldn't be interested. I didn't have any close gay friends to call. Nevertheless, I retained a certain uneasy glow. Somebody was doing something that might help me in the vaguely awkward situation I was in, although I couldn't figure out how; what could I have in common with a bunch of people who spent all their time hanging around queer bars?

I quickly found out when I became involved in GLF and my consciousness-raising group. But I kept it to myself; I was embarrassed, pure and simple, about admitting my homosexuality in front of straight men and women—particularly men. As I immersed myself in all the meetings, groups, newspapers, position papers of the movement, it became tedious to keep on drawing this line, but I didn't see any practical alternative. The climax of this duality came with the first anniversary of the Christopher Street riots; there had been talk of some sort of a demonstration ever since I had become involved in gay lib, but I didn't realize anything really concrete was planned until a couple of weeks before the march.

At a general meeting of the Gay Liberation Front, someone suggested that we all take some stickers and plaster them up all over the city. Only then did it sink in that something specific and extremely visible was going to happen, and that I was going to be a part of it. I was nervous from the beginning of my involvement, but this crystallized it. We—every lesbian and homosexual who wanted to—were to march from Waverly Place and Sixth Avenue, the heart of what has been termed New York's "gay ghetto," Greenwich Village, to the Mall in Central Park. Nobody knew how many people were going to turn out, or what the reception would be, or how the police would view the whole thing. There had been marches staged by the older homophile groups, notably the annual march in Philadelphia every Fourth of July to protest the exclusion of homosexuals from the armed forces, but this obviously was going to be something different. These people would not be defending anything or trying to protest any specific legislation or policy of the government; we would be simply affirming and proclaiming what we are. And we knew that, somehow, this simple affirmation of whatever it is that we are would be a deadly blow to the system that had foisted so many of its pathetic values on us.

I had participated in as many marches as the average liberal New Yorker; I had marched in the first big antiwar mass march in New York in 1967; I had gone to Washington twice, in November, 1969, and in May, 1970—both times feeling ineffectual but proud of myself; I had gone to all kinds of actions sponsored by schools, professional groups, neighborhood action groups. I was never very enthusiastic, but I felt I should be doing *something* to protest what was going on. The vague feeling of unease, of somehow being in the wrong place, that plagued me at these demonstrations I laid to the general malaise that was affecting the country. Of course I belonged here. If not here, where else could I go?

Now I was realizing that I had been right to feel uneasy, that I did *not* belong at those demonstrations, because I had never really felt that I should be with all those other people. They were straight, and I was not. If they knew that I had sex with other men, they would not like me and would not want me to participate in their demonstrations. This may or may not have been true; what is important is that I really did feel that way and that my feelings were not due to any insecurity on my part. That was how I was supposed to feel.

Now I had the prospect of finally being in a demonstration where I could be myself, whatever that meant. And I was still uncomfortable. I didn't know if I really belonged here either or if this really meant any more than all the other marches and demonstrations that had led to nothing. Only now, this march was going to be some sort of irrevocable step: I was going to let the whole world know I was a queer. Obviously, the world could probably not care less, but I was still anxious. I didn't know what was going to happen, and I have always feared situations I could not control.

So I made up my own controls. I decided I would march, but I left little clauses in my mind, which provided me with easy outs. If I didn't feel good, I wouldn't go. If there was any violence, I would drop out—can't condone violence. If the march was going to include too many effeminate men or butch women, I would drop out, because the march wouldn't be representative enough of the homosexuals I have encountered. As usual, events took their own course, and all my little reservations were quickly discarded, along with a lot of sturdy notions. When a friend called me and asked if I wanted to be a marshal, my instinctive and immediate answer was no. He asked me why not. When I had no good answer, he proceeded with a quick lecture on what the hell was the matter; if I wasn't willing to *do* anything, then why was I in the goddam movement anyway? I had no good answer for that either, so I very reluctantly agreed to be a marshal. I had little idea what marshals were, except that they wore armbands and were usually very officious.

So now, not only was I going to be in the parade, I was going to help run it. I couldn't imagine how that would work out, so I put the whole question out of my mind until the night before the march, when there was supposed to be a training session for marshals at Alternate U. I went very reluctantly that night and was not encouraged to discover a few people milling around who seemed to be as tentative as I was about the whole thing. We finally assembled in a large room, and then the pace picked up. A man and a woman I had never seen before were evidently instructors of some sort. They had had a lot of experience at demonstrations, and they presented us with practically every possible alternative for problems that could arise in the course of the march. I presumed they were gay, although they certainly didn't fit the stereotypes I was so worried about. Both were young, vigorous but not excitable, with the sort of humorless good humor one associates with industrious radicals. But they were very responsive to each of us, drawing us out about our particular worries and trying to make us confident about our ability to deal with hostile situations most of us had never dreamed we would encounter. I later found out that the man and woman were not—to anyone's knowledge—gay. They were part of a Quaker group that concentrated solely on training people for group actions. That was the first time I had seen straight people acknowledge gay people as gay and continue to function and to work with them, while never losing sight of or trying to ignore their homosexuality.

After a few hours of simulating hostile situations (a rather enjoyable game—it was odd to feel that one was on the side of order, for a change), we got our final instructions and maps, which described where to assemble, and agreed to meet the next morning, a few hours before the march. I was nervous that night; when I was on my first peace march, people had thrown eggs and even a bucket of paint at us, so God only knew what would happen here. Besides, there would probably be a lot of photographers there. Of course I wasn't ashamed of what I was doing, but, if my picture got in the paper, it could cause problems at my job. And I felt I had to consider these things. It took months before I realized that these concerns were pointless, that there was nothing incompatible about my homosexual experiences and every other aspect of my life. But lifelong habits are very hard to break, and my isolation of my sexuality was my most deep-rooted habit.

It was a nice day, a little chilly, when I got up. As I walked across the Village to the assembly point, through the empty early Sunday morning streets, I had one last twinge of nervousness. It seemed to be so much trouble, and I certainly didn't know what I was going to get out of it. It would be so much easier and nicer to just go for a walk by myself, as I had done on so many other sunny, bored Sundays. But I had given my word, and so I went to the assembly room.

My own qualms were dwarfed by the confusion that morning. There were scores of marshals milling around, exchanging last-minute instructions, rumors, emergency phone numbers for medical and legal aid. I spotted a familiar face and joined a group of marshals with a young man from my consciousness-raising group. We were supposed to work in these groups throughout the march if possible; each group was assigned a staging area, and we were to get there as soon as possible to hand out leaflets and explain what was going on to the people who were already arriving. Then we were to walk on the outskirts of the march as it proceeded uptown, trying to avoid as much traffic confusion as possible, and deal quickly and quietly with any troublemakers. When my group got downtown, there were only a few people behind the sawhorses, but there were a lot of police, more than I had seen assembled for any march except the biggest demonstrations. That bothered me, and their attitude bothered me even more. Many seemed to think it was funny, and even from a distance you could get the intent of the put-downs. But several policemen also came over and asked for leaflets and read them.

Some questioned us about what we were doing in this thing, how long had we been in the movement, what were the specific goals of this demonstration, and so on. I remember thinking how upset the more radical pig-hating members of GLF would be to see us consorting with our oppressors so easily. But the cops were interested, and, if anybody's attitude could be changed, a cop was as good a convert as any.

We had arrived downtown at about 10:00 A.M. Most of the passersby were still churchgoers on their way home, older people who generally gave us a suspicious once over and kept going. Occasionally some sweet old lady would ask us what we were handing out, and, with some trepidation, we would give her a flyer. Oddly enough, none ever seemed to be upset; a little puzzled, but they were ladies and so were not ruffled by people so foreign to them. The few older men who glanced at the flyers reacted much more strongly; their mouths invariably compressed into a thin line, and they shoved the flyer back without looking at us. A few people had started to assemble behind the barricades when I felt a hand on my shoulder and heard a woman's voice ask inquis-itively, "John?"

I turned around, startled, and saw a woman I worked with; she took a flyer and looked at it. She smiled at me, said good luck, and impulsively touched my shoulder again before continuing on her way with her friend. I was dumfounded; here was somebody from my office, and now she *knows*, and everyone else is going to know, and things are really going to get weird. But I didn't feel depressed; in fact, I was almost elated. Now it was all beginning to come together; even if I wanted to, there was no way I could hide anything. Now we would see what happens when the truth finally did out. Of course, like most melodramatic confrontations, this little meeting turned out to be no confrontation at all. This woman and I were friends. She was, I found out later, surprised but not shocked or horrified. It really didn't affect her opinion of me, it simply added more information to our friendship. The significant reaction was mine; I had become so conditioned to hiding what I was ashamed of that I could not believe it would not make any difference if an acquaintance casually discovered my homosexuality. Liberation or no liberation, I still took myself and my concerns very seriously, as I had always been instructed to do.

Events speeded up quickly after that. I remember only isolated vivid incidents, like stop-action frames in a movie. A lot of people arrived all at once, and it got warmer and warmer. Many of the neighborhood residents were standing in the shade watching, but after a while it was impossible to tell the onlookers from the participants. There was never meant to be much organization anyway, so the milling crowd just sort of grew imperceptibly until there were about six thousand people in the general vicinity. A lot of newspeople were there, including network cameramen, and suddenly the dilemma of what would happen if you were shown on TV faded away and was replaced by the more urgent alarm at what the newspeople were doing. Reporters and cameramen were trying to find the most extravagantly dressed transvestites and encouraging them to make sweeping statements that could provide some amusing copy when quoted out of context. Most of the newspeople ignored the march's organizers or refused to talk with them when bystanders accused them of exploiting the marchers. But the technique backfired; the media were only interested in *moderately* outrageous people, and the street queens were anything but moderate. When they wanted to put on a show, they could; very little of their indignation and acidly funny diatribes could be used on television or quoted in family newspapers. So the reporters were left with the perhaps duller but more acceptable homosexuals as their focus.

We were finally ready to move out, and the mood of the group, a little frantic and nervous from the beginning, sud-

denly became serious. There were a lot of cops and a lot of
bystanders along the first few blocks. Sixth Avenue is a very
broad, straight thoroughfare; there are a few swells, so periodically you could get out of the line of march and see how
big the parade really was. We stayed in the far left lane, close
to the curb; the function of the marshals was to make sure
that there wasn't any obstruction of traffic, so that we
wouldn't get a fine or worse. I kept scanning the faces of the
people along the curb. There was almost no overt hostility.
Surprisingly enough, there were several familiar faces, homosexuals who evidently did not feel interested or committed
enough to march. But the great majority of onlookers were
men and women out for a Sunday walk; their reaction was
startled incomprehension.

As we moved quickly uptown, there were fewer people
looking at us, but there were still all kinds of reactions. Several carloads of young people roared alongside, shouting
encouragement. That was a surprise. We raced past empty
gleaming skyscrapers and dilapidated brownstones. Occasionally a head would stick out of a window, and from one
building a group of hairy freaks screamed encouragement.
There was nobody to protect us from, and some of the police
looked a little disappointed, but they kept pushing us, trying
to get us off the street as soon as possible.

The feelings that flickered through my head as we sped
along were vague, yet intense and new. I was doing something with a bunch of strangers, shouting slogans and impreca-
tions that I had never used and really couldn't take seriously.
"Out of the closets and into the streets." "Two, four,
six, eight, gay is just as good as straight." "Ho-ho-homosexual,
the ruling class is ineffectual." But they *were* true, they had
to be said. I never stopped feeling embarrassed, and yet I
have never regretted or minimized anything I did that day. I
couldn't get used to that juxtaposition of acute embarrassment and the need for those same embarrassing actions. What

I finally realized was that the two were not exclusive of one another, and, at any rate, the cause for embarrassment lay in my social conditioning, rather than any concrete thing I actually did. I had been told for so long that my "secret" life was wrong, that I was naturally embarrassed at first. At first.

When we finally arrived at Central Park, there was another crowd assembled; they were even more puzzled, because they hadn't received the heavy barrage of stickers and posters that had covered the Village for the past month. Moreover, the high degree of eccentricity tolerated and even encouraged in the Village was glaringly incongruous in Central Park, that haven of retired folks, family outings, and hip young married couples. But the momentum of the march deterred any possible adverse reaction. We swept right through to the Sheep Meadow, picking up a few more converts.

When we finally stopped, we were on a little hill. I remember everyone turning around at once to see the end of the march straggle in and everyone realizing that this wasn't the end, that there were hundreds of people still pouring in. It was a simple, concrete, and somehow unbelievable fact— there were so *many* of us. There really is strength in numbers; I didn't understand exactly how, but there certainly was something bigger than any individual going on here. I looked around, saw a lot of familiar faces, and many, many new ones. I didn't feel any more or less warm or hostile toward them; my attractions and dislikes weren't undergoing any radical alterations. Rather, I realized that *we* were all in this together, that at that particular moment I *should* be in that place rather than any other.

The inevitable confusion of any large gathering took over very soon. Now that we were here, what were we going to do? Oddly enough, I hadn't really considered this; I had been so preoccupied with dodging imaginary bottles and epithets that I had never thought of what was going to happen once you

got several thousand homosexuals in one place. Now I saw
—a sort of gentle chaos that was more tolerant than any other
large gathering I had ever seen. It reminded me of those
pompous, flowery, but somehow touching descriptions of San
Francisco and the first love-ins of the mid-1960's. There were
large and small groups forming all over the enormous field,
some just talking, some performing all kinds of group activities, from the standard physical encounter games that one
could see every weekend in the park, to group chants and
kissing-endurance contests. The friend who had accompanied
me quickly grew bored and decided to leave, so I wandered
about for a few hours by myself. I was bored, too, I had to
admit, and I felt slightly guilty about it. How could this be
such a good thing, such a big deal, and still be boring? I felt
the old malaise returning: why wasn't I more *involved*?

It was very sunny that afternoon, but not too warm; the
kind of rare summer afternoon that keeps people from leaving New York for good. I ran into several people that I had
met in the GLF and my consciousness-raising group; they all
looked happy, but they said the same things that I was feeling—"Is this it? Why doesn't something *happen*?" We were
a little disappointed that this was all there was; and yet it
really was so much. No leaders, no organization, just us and
our—whatever it was—our cause, our beliefs. As I watched
two young men kissing—somebody said they had been doing
it for over an hour—I heard stray bits of conversation; none
concerned the issues of gay liberation. People were still talking about what their friends had done last night, and other
people's clothes, and what they were going to have for dinner,
and who was that fantastic person over there. We had made
our gesture, and that was what it was, in the end. A gesture,
not a summation, or a proof. As I walked away from the
kissing contest—which was beginning to resemble a side
show, complete with ice cream-hawkers—I saw a little family
group approaching—mother, father, two little girls. They

didn't look like Manhattanites; they were probably Irish or Italian or Polish, from the Bronx or Brooklyn or Queens. And they were definitely enjoying the show; or at least the parents were, shoving each other in the ribs when they figured out what was going on on the ground behind all those people. The little girls looked tired and confused.

This whole march was for us, for homosexuals to express themselves; but there we were, in Central Park, surrounded by smiling, hard-working people on their day off who viewed us as a sort of side show that had nothing to do with their lives. As I walked across the field to leave, I saw these thousands of men and women, sitting or lying around in groups, some walking from one group to another. The swirling masses that had earlier covered the field were now dispersed into these little groups, quietly looking at each other. I was glad that the march had come off well, with no violence; but it was such a small beginning compared to what we were facing, what we had to do. These groups of quiet, half-smiling, somewhat bewildered young women and men were going to try to change the whole direction of Western culture. They were going to take on the Bible, the U.S. Government, an army of psychiatrists, their own families, the media, the radical establishment, and even hidden aspects of themselves.

Just at the edge of the Sheep Meadow, away from most of the marchers, a TV crew had set up to get reactions from the park's Sunday regulars. The interviewer was talking to a boy of about eighteen, who was wearing a worn football jersey; the boy was big, and dark-haired, with a bulldog jaw. He looked like some southern cousins of mine that I had always admired and feared a little as a child; walking nearer, I heard that the boy actually did have a southern accent. The announcer talked to his cameraman for a moment and then turned back to the boy and asked him, with a knowing smirk, "Well, what do *you* think of all this?"

I never saw the interview on television, and I wasn't taking notes, so I didn't get the exact reply. But I remember the thoughtful frown that creased the boy's forehead as he shifted uneasily and finally said, "Well . . . these people are pretty strange to me. But, you know, they should do what they want." I also remember the interviewer's disgusted sigh as he signaled the cameramen to wrap it up; this obviously wasn't going to be good stuff. And I remember the boy's probably impulsive, but extremely important, distinction: "These people" should not be *allowed* to do what they want. They should just do it.

5 disillusion and alternatives

THE MARCH TO Central Park was the most striking demonstration of unity among homosexuals that I have yet encountered. But, even in the march, there were troubling divisions and imbalances. It was primarily a white, middle-class, and radical-academic coalition, the same formula that dominates most protest groups in this country. The question of participation by third-world people in the gay liberation movement was just as thorny here as elsewhere. Less striking, but perhaps even more dangerous, was the continuing separation of men and women. Despite their common labels of queer and homosexual, gay women and men were often openly hostile to one another and derisive of those who were particularly "fem" or "butch." In the Gay Liberation Front, this hos-

106

tility and fear was confronted over and over; the source was always found to be the sexual stereotypes that we have all been saddled with and are now attempting to overthrow. But the separation persisted, in its most visible forms, even during the march; when the parade arrived at the park, the men formed into groups and so did the women. There was very little communication. There was work to do, and the women and men could do that together. But their problems and interests were different, and there was very little to be done about that right now.

This contradiction between the ideal and the hard facts of our situation was brought home most clearly by an incident that happened a few weeks after the march. At a Sunday night GLF meeting, during a particularly dull stretch of proceedings, a black transvestite got up and told how she had been forced to leave a gay bar in the East Village the night before. The reaction to her story was at first a little apprehensive, because, at that stage, the Gay Liberation Front was just beginning to confront the phenomenon of transvestitism in the gay community. Many homosexuals who were not obvious homosexuals, and who had worked hard to make sure that they were not obvious, had just begun to be honest about their own sexuality. In this precarious position, they felt threatened by the drag queens, men who seemed to take on the most feminine aspects of the woman's role and to submit voluntarily to the problems a woman must go through. Moreover, the transvestites were usually highly aggressive, flirting and joking; they could be extremely articulate and were often hilariously funny. None of these traits reassured the men who were trying to keep their homosexuality in its proper place.

While the drag queen, whose name was Nova, told us about the incident, the mood of the room rapidly changed; looking back, I am even more confused now than I was then. Nova seemed to me to be—by *her* choice—more woman than man, in every way. I wondered if I was responding to her dilemma in the way that a man responds to a woman in trouble, or if I was acting in response to the real and outrageous facts of the situation; I still have not solved this strange dilemma.

According to her account, Nova had been in the Hip-o-Drome the previous night when the owner approached her and told her to leave. After some heated discussion, during which she was told that there didn't have to be any reason for her to be thrown out, Nova finally left. She exaggerated, condemned, exhorted, and generally carried on like a classic movie queen; but it was obvious that she was hurt and angry. Gay bars were supposedly made for people to be themselves in; if she could be summarily thrown out, then she was in even more trouble than she had thought. And, she rightly added, so were we.

This touched a sore point. Bars, at least in New York, have always been the principal social focus of gay life. Yet everyone that I have talked to who frequents bars has had complaints about them. They are not places of relaxation or friendship; they are arenas. Prices are high; crowding is often intolerable; the people who own them often treat you like freaks. The few exceptions, where patrons are considered human beings, usually become so jammed that the bar becomes a target for a takeover by the Mafia, which owns virtually all gay bars in New York City. This particular bar was notorious. The owner was often rude; waiters pushed you to drink; and beer cost a dollar a bottle. But it was the only all-gay bar in the East Village and one of the few places that allowed dancing. A lot of East Village radical gay people went there, even at a dollar a beer. It's hard to fight capitalism when you're lonesome or horny. But nobody really liked the place; anyone who had a good time did so against all odds. Besides, if the place was crowded enough, you could get away without buying a beer.

Nova's experience was seized upon enthusiastically as a

reason for confronting this place and the people who ran it. She asked that we help her by staging some sort of demonstration to protest their arbitrary oppression of any customer they didn't care for. Several people suggested that we go down there at once, and so we did. I was amazed, exhilarated, and very nervous. This was it, real confrontation, not a peaceful march but an attack on a place that was fucking us over. About seventy-five people marched from the church to the bar, a distance of about twenty-five blocks. I was with some people I didn't know very well; as we talked on the way down, I was suddenly reminded of college and people with whom I had only been able to talk about classes that we had shared. Here we were talking about our sexual predilections and our status as an oppressed class; but the caution, the rather touching formality with which we faced each other was still there.

I remember particularly one fragment of conversation with a woman who has done much for the liberation of women and all gay people. She is an imposing person, with a brilliant mind and an angry, sharp tongue. That night, she seemed to be almost as nervous and yet exhilarated as a novice like me. I tried to talk with her about some writing she had done on the position of Panthers in relation to gay liberation. Her thinking seemed to be more integrated with her life and work than mine, and I think she was hard-pressed to explain what seemed to her self-evident truths. The remark that impressed me most was that *the* revolution, the total change in life styles as well as politics, must not be simply something to do for middle-class people. It was not an occupation or an amusement, to be picked up or dropped at will. You had to realize that if you were going to be in it, you had better be all the way in it, or stay out. I thought a lot about what she had said in the weeks that followed. The revolution wasn't a matter of what you said, or how much violence you promised. It was what you were.

Her remarks, it turned out, were in ironic contrast to the

events that night. A large group assembled in front of the Hip-o-Drome and tried to enter; there was some business with baseball bats and bouncers at the door, and several squad cars quickly showed up. We were told to march in a sort of large circle, and so we did, shouting the now familiar chants. As we passed the bar, we could see the angry staff inside and the puzzled, amused, or frightened patrons of the bar. Occasionally a few customers would scurry out, to be greeted by shouts of abuse or welcome, depending on whether they fled or stayed to join the protest. The bar's owner was not there, none of the staff would talk to us, perhaps because we had no clearly designated leader, and so the march continued on and on. My nervousness and exhilaration quickly turned to boredom. Being a radical homosexual was okay, but I still had my bourgeois job, where I unfortunately had to show up at 9 A.M.

Meanwhile, the neighborhood was stirring. The Hip-o-Drome is situated in the East Village, with a large Puerto Rican and black population, as well as many old people who have remained from the earlier Ukrainian settlements. The local people were aware of this bar in their midst, but they had ignored it. They were not pleased to find a parade of angry homosexuals shouting outside it at midnight on a Sunday night. Out of the corner of my eye I noticed a group forming across the street, and soon people were shouting at us, telling us to get out and making the usual jokes. A little later, I heard a crash, and then a few more as bottles exploded on the sidewalk around us.

I was scared now, in a totally nonintellectual way. This was not a real public demonstration; we were a small group of people in a hostile neighborhood, shouting late at night about grievances no one but us felt. The cops stood around, looking even more unreal in the glaring fluorescent lights that made the street glow with an ugly false daylight. Marchers were now telling us to watch out for these cops, they were about to make their move; others were warning us of provocateurs in our midst who were trying to start violence. People that I had seen espouse the most drastic actions in meetings were calmly and efficiently trying to keep the demonstration going, without its turning into a rout or melting away. But other people, most of whom I had never seen before, were screaming hysterically at cops, screaming at the closed doors of the bar.

Then the most confusing event of the night occurred. A few radical GLF men went over to the neighborhood people gathered across the street and tried to explain what we were doing. They were greeted with derisive shouts and laughter, but they raised their voices and kept going. I remember thinking that they really were brave. Then I listened to their reasons for our action, and I became even more confused. They told how a black man had been refused service at the bar, and how we were here in sympathy with him. But Nova did not, as far as I could tell, think of herself as a black man; I certainly didn't know what she thought of herself as, but to simplify her identity into "a black man" seemed to be a real distortion of what she was attempting to do with her life. These men were attempting to radicalize the crowd, but at what cost? All of a sudden, I was in deep enough to start worrying about ideological purity. I found myself now siding with a feared specter—the drag queen—against anyone who wanted to make her acceptable. I felt some idea was asserting itself, but I didn't know how or where it would lead me.

After an hour or so, the demonstrators began to tire and the police became more insistent that we leave, so we all assembled in a park a couple of blocks from the bar. I was tired and still very nervous; I was beginning to understand the paranoia that radical people feel around the police. The fact that *everything* I was doing stood against *everything* that they were doing made it all too possible that they would swoop down on us and cart us off to a jail where we would never be heard from again. During our brief meeting in the park, everyone kept glancing nervously about. We agreed to call a meeting that Tuesday, formulate a plan of action against the Hip-o-Drome, and perhaps get started on a comprehensive campaign to establish an alternative to gay bars, or to radicalize the ones that now existed. Then, with an audible sigh of relief, we left the meeting and went our separate ways. Some people were disappointed that the confrontation hadn't been more meaningful (that is, more dramatic, more violent, more clearly defined, more something), but we all assumed that this was just a beginning and we could handle these problems as they came up.

That, as it turned out, was quite an assumption. I didn't go to the meeting that Tuesday night, so perhaps I cannot fairly criticize the results of whatever happened. I didn't patronize bars, and, although I did feel that there were a lot of things radically wrong with the way people related to one another in those bars, I didn't think my experience was wide enough for me to say anything about the situation much beyond conjecture. I thought that those people who had been most vocal at the demonstration would be at least equally vocal at the meeting. That was a mistake on my part; one should never expect anyone to do the work that one doesn't want to.

The meeting was not well-attended that night; the owner of the bar came by and evidently made some statement about the whole incident's being a misunderstanding. The outcome was that no concrete steps against the Hip-o-Drome would be taken. All the talk about boycotts, leafleting, forcing bar owners to meet the demands of the gay community—all were immediately forgotten. I was disappointed and angry when I heard that. I hadn't marched around for a couple of hours, feeling like a fool and yet believing in what I was nervously shouting, just for the hell of it. I had wanted my actions to mean something, to change some little part of the rigid system

I kept running up against. Evidently we had made some sort of impact; the owner did show up, after all. But why hadn't someone insisted that he answer all those demands of the community that we had talked about; why hadn't we used all that angry energy to achieve something concrete? When I voiced my dissatisfaction, someone rightly told me to shut up, since I hadn't seen fit to do anything about it myself.

After a while I realized that this was a more painful example of the phenomenon that had happened after the march reached Central Park. Now that we are here, what are we going to do? We were not really prepared for success; despite all the talk, the actuality of creating new life styles was incredibly difficult work, perhaps even impossible. And it would take a lot more than one confrontation over one crummy bar to do it.

I became rapidly more cynical about the possibilities of this particular group achieving any action that was meaningful to *me*. But I soon learned that they had already done a lot. For example, one of the first protests staged by the Gay Liberation Front was directed against the *Village Voice*, which has become the *New York Times* of hip New Yorkers. The *Voice*, although by far the most liberal of the major New York papers, consistently referred to women as chicks, to homosexual men as fags, fairies, et cetera, and to lesbians as dykes. They did not call black people niggers or Italians wops; they wouldn't have gotten away with it, and, besides, everyone knew *racial* slurs were a bad thing. The GLF mounted a demonstration demanding that the *Voice* stop using derogatory language in articles that mentioned homosexuals, that the word "gay" be allowed to appear in ads, that homosexuals be allowed to advertise homosexual gatherings, parties, dances, and so on with as much honesty as heterosexuals, that homosexuals be allowed to advertise for roommates openly, that events in the homosexual community be covered fully. The demonstration worked. The *Voice* has become, somewhat reluctantly, a major source of news for and about homosexuals; it is particularly valuable for those readers outside large cities who don't have access to gay periodicals. It is still disconcerting to read, in every issue, about fags or dykes, and to see individuals' sexual preferences held up as objects of derision and proofs of general incompetence. Moreover, the *Voice* kindly gave space to its film-reviewer, Andrew Sarris (an admitted authority on movies but self-admittedly completely ignorant of homosexual experiences) to state, in explicit and rather boring detail, why gay liberation had gone too far. In other words, the *Voice* may have to print things about homosexuals but it doesn't have to like them.

There were other protests, against bars and shop-owners, and there were leaflets and position papers. There was a colorful, noisy demonstration on Forty-Second Street; there were solidarity demonstrations with the Panthers, with various radical women's groups; there were group trips to the Revolutionary Peoples' Constitutional Convention in Philadelphia and to a similar event in Washington. I participated in only one of the above; the rest I heard about by hearsay and garbled accounts in the press, both gay and straight. The one event I did participate in—the march on Forty-Second Street—convinced me that I and a lot of other homosexuals were never going to be comfortable in mass actions.

A protest had been called to demand the end of police harassment of homosexuals on Forty-Second Street. A bit of background for those unfamiliar with Forty-Second Street: it is no longer Busby Berkeley's Street of Dreams. It is an ugly, crowded, flashy stretch of theaters, amusement arcades, pornographic bookstores, and pizza parlors. Homosexuals frequent many of the theaters and provide customers for the bookstores, many of which have far more material meant for homosexuals than heterosexuals. The emphasis here, as in all of New York, is on making as many bucks as possible with the smallest outlay. These exploitative attractions lure large crowds, which necessitate large numbers of cops to handle them. In the summer of 1970, among all the prostitution, pimping, drug traffic, con games, watered drinks, strippers, and $5 sex movies, the police chose to start running in homosexuals—not hustlers, but anyone who looked homosexual. To their surprise, the police netted several otherwise solid young citizens, who protested vociferously. This demonstration was called to protest that harassment and at the same time condemn the entire exploitative sex industry that kept the street so greasily prosperous.

Once again, things got very confused very fast. There were several hundred people assembled by the time the march finally got under way—half an hour late. There were carloads of police, but only a few cameramen and only a small crowd of onlookers. We were a block away from the street's center of activity, and, as we finally started marching toward the double row of flashing marquees, I got the feeling that I was being drawn into something—some giant pinball machine in which we would all be so many little cartoon figures flashing on and off. The feeling didn't go away.

There were a lot of people out, and they stood back to let us pass, but they didn't seem to be really seeing us; we were part of the scene, no more or less interesting or objectionable than the crudely tinted pictures outside the theaters. I noticed a group of swaggering men, all of them about thirty years old and dressed in new levis, polo shirts, prominently displayed peace symbols, and short hair. They were alternating their swaggering with mincing imitations of what straight people must have thought of homosexuals thirty years ago. Suddenly it flashed through my mind—these were real, honest-to-God plainclothesmen. I was a little disappointed; they certainly weren't very good at it. They weren't trying to infiltrate at all; in fact, they never left their little group. They didn't look like any of the real street people that surrounded them; in fact, they didn't look like any homo-

sexuals I had ever seen. They looked ugly and stupid and—
now I realized that I should be worried, not disappointed
—very cruel.

I was shocked again to discover that the people we had
come to save certainly didn't want us and, in their minds at
least, didn't need us. A few paces in front of me, some sort
of fight had started, providing much amusement to the onlookers and plainclothesmen. Evidently, the assailant was one
of the street's regulars—a once pretty man of about thirty-
five, with carefully sprayed hair and a carefully color-coor-
dinated outfit; he had collared one of the marchers, a Village
long hair in jeans, sandals, and work shirt, and was hissing
at him with incredible ferocity. "Why don't you get the fuck
out? You're ruining it for *us*! Why don't you just get out?"
He was immediately bombarded with answers from all sides,
telling him to come into the streets, liberate himself, and
throw off the bonds of sexist oppression.

But he was right, of course; I suddenly felt very foolish
and a little tired. If people are homosexuals, if homosexuality becomes the defining factor of their lives, they may
still have great differences in life styles, politics, even clothes.
We had come up from the Village to show these people a
thing or two, and now we were going right back. What had
we changed? How had we offered that man—whose life
frightened and saddened and fascinated me—any real alternative? We were making fun of what he had struggled to get
to, and he hated us for it, and I couldn't blame him.

We were marching faster now, already a little bored with
this. This was no crusade, like the march on Sixth Avenue;
it was becoming one more show on a whole row of shows, all
of them about sex. We weren't making any impression. As
we went by a newsstand, I smelled tear gas. Only a few of
us noticed it, evidently, and the recriminations against the
police quickly stopped when it was evident that they hadn't
done it. I looked at the little old man hidden behind his rows

of newspapers in the stand we had just passed. He was smiling slightly; he probably did it, I thought. He's like everyone else up here, making money from homosexuals and despising them. And the homosexuals let it happen, because they need this world. And they, we, have no alternative yet.

We made a circuit of both sides of the busiest block on Forty-Second Street four or five times, and then everyone got simultaneously disgusted and decided to do something else. The disagreement was over what the next course of action would be; feeling guilty and immensely relieved, I said I had to meet a friend for dinner since I hadn't eaten all day (the truth), and so I couldn't go on with them to their next objective. I met my friend, and we had a good Chinese dinner. As I drifted off to sleep that night, I heard sirens and wondered fancifully if there was finally a gay revolution.

There was a serious attempt going on, as it turned out. Most of the marchers had gone on to the police station that was the center of the Forty-Second Street harassment and spent some time chanting, with no real response. Then they had marched down to the Village, to the intersection of Greenwich Avenue and Christopher Street, a few doors away from the famous Stonewall, scene of the first gay riots; across the street from the intersection was the notorious Women's House of Detention. And the riots of the previous year were re-enacted. Not with the shocked joyousness that came when homosexuals first realized their potential strength, but with the angry desperation of people who had been fighting a long time. I wasn't there; I only talked to people who had been there and saw a few who had been hurt; one man's scalp was ripped brutally in several places; another had his arm broken; several were arrested and beaten by the police. I went to the GLF meeting the next night, and we once again marched off to the scene of the previous night's troubles.

I had told myself that I would not let myself get involved in mass protests if I weren't comfortable, and here I was again. But I had to *see*, I had to figure out the direction of what was going on. There were several homophile groups there, including relatively conservative ones who quickly put away their identifying banners when the police arrived, which was within minutes after the GLF contingent got there. We then began an elaborate ballet, moving from one end of the block to the other, going around the block, down alleys. Periodically a line of cops advanced, the dreaded TPF (the Tactical Police Force, the bane of New York's radical demonstrators). They would advance, sometimes slowly, sometimes quickly, slapping their billy clubs against their gloved palms, their baby-blue helmets glowing in the dark. We would advance and retreat correspondingly, shouting abuse but trying to keep well out of the way of the clubs with which they occasionally poked people.

This went on for an hour or so. A friend and I, both bored and a little scared, stepped out of line and went into a coffee shop (one of the conveniences of demonstrating in crowded New York). I once again voiced my misgivings: the cops were going to arrest us; the protest was pointless; people could get hurt; we were alienating potential fellow liberationists. He said that, even if all that were true, the mob scene had to go on because the time was right; the homosexuals who were marching outside were not being rational, they were acting out of their instincts, and that was good and true, and to hell with the consequences. As we joined the march, a few bottles from out of nowhere exploded near us. I thought, here goes. Whether it's angry demonstrators or hostile neighborhood people, the shit is going to fly.

I waited, but it didn't for a while, and so I started to leave after another fifteen minutes. Suddenly I saw another large contingent swinging in from a new direction. Talking to people in the group, I heard that O'Henry's, a popular and expensive tourist steak house, had had its sidewalk cafe disrupted. I was shocked; gay people were right in there with the Weathermen, destroying the ruling class. I had had a good steak at O'Henry's once, and I felt a little sorry for the place; but it was somehow appropriate. All those people who came to absorb the atmosphere created by freaks were now finding out what freaks were really like. But I didn't want to hurt anybody, or even take a chance. Though I could understand the action, I couldn't really encourage it. I decided to slip out and go home, the course of least resistance.

I went by O'Henry's to see the damage. There was hardly any, but there were unusually few customers and through the glass I saw the manager gesticulating violently. Whatever had been done wasn't that bad, despite the panicky exultation of the gays I had just seen. The ruling class is able to absorb a lot. There were a few arrests that night, I heard later, and I noticed that, for a few weeks, the West Village was even more tense than usual, but angry demonstrations seemed to have played themselves out for a while.

• • •

The most dramatic, the most unsuccessful, and the most far-reaching confrontation came several weeks later, in mid-September, when the gay community of Greenwich Village took on New York University, the educational behemoth, situated in the heart of the Village, that was patiently buying up and converting large areas of the Village for its own uses. NYU had inadvertently played host to the Gay Activists' Alliance the night of the Christopher Street Liberation Day parade. That group had reserved an enormous hall in the subcellar of NYU's most modern dormitory; here, in this rather elegant air-conditioned vault, far below ground level, where all possible noise could be absorbed, GAA held an enormously successful dance. By the time NYU officials found out who was using their hall, the dance was under way. Later, the planning group that had put together the march leased the hall for a series of dances from the student governing board, which determined who should get to use the hall. Two dances were successfully held; they were well-attended, inexpensive, carefully planned so that women would not be outnumbered or abused, laid out so that people could congregate in groups or easily move into less crowded areas. The large profits shown by the dances were being put back into more dances and more community events.

As the school year started, however, returning officials took one look at what was going on and demanded that the whole thing stop. NYU—founded as a Methodist institution and still highly moralistic at the administrative and trustee levels —demanded that the dances stop. When the contract was mentioned, officials said students had no right to negotiate contracts if the administration disagreed. When several hundred people showed up for a dance that had been advertised long in advance of NYU's ban, the doors were locked and security guards demanded that those waiting for the dance leave. Another riot nearly erupted, until one lone official ventured in, a few hours later, to open the doors and allow the remaining angry homosexuals into a bare, silent hall, where they milled around for a while and finally left.

The next step was a sit-in. Called by people from various radical homosexual groups, it happened quickly, with only a dozen or so people participating. The Gay Liberation Front called out thirty of forty available bodies, and the sit-in began in earnest. I heard about this the next day, although the dorm is only a block or so from where I live. Despite the fact that a minority group was challenging a bigoted policy of a major educational institution, I hadn't heard a word about the occupation in the press. I was very excited as I went over to NYU that afternoon: at last, a really meaningful struggle. NYU was one of the most important forces in the city; to confront it on the issue of homosexuality would finally bring out a lot of the serious issues that we had until now only tentatively explored.

But, as I entered the subcellar, where the sit-ins were congregating, I realized once and for all that "we" was illusory. There were a lot of individuals on one side against an anonymous institution on the other, and I could not feel any strong alliance between myself and these other individuals, although in the eyes of that anonymous institution we were all an undesirable moral influence on "impressionable" underclassmen.

I had always envisioned sit-ins as being some sort of serious camping out, with a lot of camaraderie and an underlying serious purpose that somehow made the whole event touching and meaningful. I remembered the blacks who had sat in at white lunch counters in the South, and their impassive, noble dismissal of the incredible abuse that was being thrown at them. I also remembered TV accounts of the students who had nearly overthrown Columbia University; they seemed excited, almost joyful, turning a political act into a sort of psychodrama where the father figure was once and for all smashed. But the gay people sitting in at NYU were the first group I had ever actually *seen* in an occupied building, and they were not happy, or noble, or brave. They were tired, dirty, strident, and hostile. All my doubts were finally solidified: what in the hell was I doing here?

I looked around to see if there was anyone I knew; there wasn't. People were in small groups, each group scattered far from the others about the huge room. As I tried to circle the room unobtrusively and get involved in *something*, I heard someone in each group holding forth on some political rap. I was at once impressed and discouraged; these people were talking about the revolution, about what was going to happen after the revolution, about what to do when the police finally came. And I was looking for something interesting to do; I didn't want to stay in some huge, empty room way below ground, lit by long fluorescent bulbs. I just wanted to see what was going on. There were a lot of transvestites there, many black people, many women; there wasn't any of the almost boy-scout atmosphere that often predominated in the mostly white, mostly male meetings. It was a difficult job they were doing, very messy and tiring, with little chance of any successful outcome that would be more than symbolic. It was so difficult that I couldn't even imagine myself doing it. And for that I felt guilty.

Suddenly there was a flurry of activity as some new people arrived. The students who lived in the building, and who were supposed to decide who got to use the hall, had been talking on and off with the gay people; now residents of each floor wanted to talk with the gay people and vote on whether they supported the sit-in. I was really curious to see the inter-action between these "impressionable" underclassmen and the street homosexuals who had invaded their dorm. But it was important that each floor be sent a representative sample of the occupiers, and there wasn't any room for the merely curious.

I stuck my head in a few times during the remainder of the occupation, which lasted for five days and five nights, but I never stayed very long. I certainly agreed in principle with what was going on and was delighted and fascinated by the spectacle of the NYU machine, supposedly dedicated to education, fighting so desperately to keep out any new ideas or "undesirable" influences. But my level of commitment was simply not strong enough to let me put my condition, my middle-class self-image, my pride, behind me and dig in.

Finally, the entire issue was resolved, unfortunately from above. The students had given a somewhat reluctant, con-fused, but definitely anti-police vote of support for the sit-in. There was even talk of another dance. This was too much for NYU; the administration called in the TPF, which was rapidly becoming the principal opponent of gay radicals. Three busloads of police piled into the dormitory, wearing those damn baby-blue helmets. They lined up, batting palms with nightsticks, and told everybody to get out. Everybody did.

I talked to several people who were there; they agreed that it was the most frightening, naked display of antihomosexual power they had seen. Backed into a corner, they had no way out but the way the police told them to go. And it would have taken very little to make the police riot. As it was, some cops were disappointed that there wasn't more commotion; they grabbed three gay people and tried to get them into a police car, letting them feel the full brunt of their fury when they tried to resist. The *New York Times* carried a small mention of the sit-in's ending, but nothing about the violence; the hip FM rock radio stations, which had somewhat incredulously reported the beginning of the sit-in, said nothing.

It seemed as though the whole sit-in had been lost in the bowels of the giant NYU machine. The great majority of New York's gay population heard nothing about the sit-in until it was long over, and then only through the notoriously late, inaccurate, and somewhat hostile commercial gay press. The *Village Voice* did devote half a page to it three weeks after the police had been called in. The gay demands—which ranged from a rather vague demand for open admissions for all gay people to requirements for discussion of homosexuality in relevant courses, encouragement of student homophile groups, and use of university facilities by the enormous gay community in which NYU is situated—were ignored. There was one course on aspects of homosexuality offered, but not for credit, during NYU's spring, 1971, term. It was a cheap price to pay for salving the conscience of a "liberal" group of academics, but it was a beginning. Despite its revolutionary implications for the academic-bourgeois ideal of happy, studious, hard-working, and fulfilled family units, the course is still being given—part and parcel of the rigid, expensive educational machine that seems to be the only way to certify the gaining of knowledge in America.

• • •

Like many other people, I was feeling more and more uncomfortable about my inability to be as political as the GLF
required. The incidents mentioned above certainly strengthened these doubts. But there were other events that showed
me how I was still strongly involved with whatever it was
that the GLF was about. The best example is what happened
at a meeting of GLF men. Proposed frankly in imitation of
GLF women's meetings, these gatherings were an attempt to
form a cohesive group-consciousness among males, just as the
women seemed to be doing among themselves. They were
also meant to be an alternative to the increasingly frantic yet
necessary focus on "business" at the Sunday night meetings.

The meetings were held in a large loft in Manhattan's
Chelsea district. The first night that I attended was in mid-
summer; although the meeting was scheduled to begin at
8:00, it was still very light when I arrived. I noted with
disbelief that the building where we were meeting also
housed the New York branch of the Communist Party as well
as the main editorial offices of *Screw* magazine, the first and
raunchiest of the underground pornographic journals. If
some rabid right-winger who equated sexual permissiveness
with pornography and left-wing politics with godless anarchy
happened to stumble on the place, he could strike a blow for
Americanism by bombing the whole building back to the
Stone Age. What he wouldn't realize was that there was as
much divergence among each of those menacing groups as
between himself and any of them.

The loft seemed incredible to me during that first meeting.
Enormous and empty except for a small, beautifully finished
kitchen standing in the middle of its space, it seemed to float
above the city. There were large windows on three sides,
with wide sills where one could sit. There were a few arm-
chairs and several cheap oriental rugs scattered over the floor
to make a checkerboard pattern. Their dark, rich colors stood
out against the pale green walls and the spots where the peel-

ing paint had been carefully sanded down to the bare white plaster beneath. The loft belonged to a fabric designer, and there were odd pieces of cloth lying in a corner and thrown across one wall that completed the effect of our being in some sort of special retreat. We were nine flights up, and, even with all the windows open, the city's noise was muted.

The first meeting was extremely tentative; we knew that not much new ground was being covered in the general meetings, and we didn't know why. I suspect that many, like myself, wondered if there really was much new ground to cover. There were a lot of personal attacks and bickering as well; the inhibitions of a large, semiorganized meeting had vanished, and many of the men let personal animosities loose that had been accumulating for months. But there was also a relaxed tone, a sort of playfulness that was absent in those larger meetings. We may have been a group of sexual revolutionaries, attempting to alter radically the social structure of society, but we were also a group of men who found each other highly attractive, and many of us were intent on showing it. The meeting broke up amid a lot of analysis about exactly what we were doing and the dangers of self-indulgence, along with a little discreet exchanging of telephone numbers. It was funny, and somehow comforting, to see this group of long hairs doing things that men do in the depressing atmosphere of gay bars, but doing them without the bravura and feigned self-assurance that make gay bars more like theaters than places where human beings can simply get together.

The next week's meeting took a little more time to get off the ground. There were a few rather stringent critiques of the last week's discussion and, after several long pauses, some suggestions on work we could do together that would make us closer. I shuddered inwardly as I imagined us all standing around an assembly line that ground out increasingly complex and boring manifestoes, declarations, position papers, decorated with "revolutionary artwork." I worked with a lot of people every day, and I certainly didn't know them very well. Would this be any different? There were more long pauses, and a few people left. I remember one man falling asleep with his head in someone's lap.

Finally a discussion got started on the comparative feasibility of two possible work projects, with the participants getting very hot under the collar and several others, like myself, eying the door and wondering if it might not be best to call it a night. One man quietly got up and went into the bathroom. When he came back, he had no clothes on. He sat down quietly where he had been before; the speakers and most of the people in the room didn't even notice what he had done.

About ten minutes later, a young man across the room started getting undressed. A few others followed suit and sat down. The speakers, still wrapped up in their dispute, began to notice that their audience's attention was quickly waning. They attempted to enlarge the discussion, but by now there were several little whispered conversations, a lot of giggling, and a general restiveness. Suddenly someone jumped up and demanded to know what the fuck was going on with these people who were trying to disrupt the meeting. The whole place exploded. People started shouting for him to shut up, for the others to get their clothes on, goddamit, and stop this foolishness, to ignore these people and let them do whatever they wanted to do. Finally someone shouted for everybody to shut up and asked the guy who had started the whole thing to explain what he was doing.

He spoke haltingly. I suddenly felt that he had really acted on impulse, that he had not given any thought to what would happen after his actions. I was impressed. He said that we had been talking too much, and only about what we were *going* to do, when it seemed that the problem was what was going on here, right now in this room. He said that he wasn't nearly as interested in his future as he was in his present and that we were not communicating, or really doing anything. We were just talking and talking.

More uproar, more people shouting about stupid and disruptive tactics some people were using, others telling the first group to shut up, others asking everyone to quiet down so the man could talk, a few more taking their clothes off. Finally things got quiet enough so that the man could finish what he was saying. He talked about how we were projecting about future events, over and over again, and how we never really made any personal decisions. And, if we wanted to be closer to one another, one very simple and immediate way of doing it would be to take off our clothes. A few people yelled that this was fascist, manipulative. He said he wasn't challenging anyone to do it, he was just asking them to make a decision, an immediate decision; either stay dressed or get undressed. But, if they got undressed, it would at least be some sort of change from the kind of people they were before.

That decided me. The people I was sitting with were eying each other somewhat nervously and fiddling with buttons. I suddenly figured what the hell and took off my clothes. Because I was only wearing jeans, a pullover, and sandals, it didn't take long. When I finished, I noticed that most of the people around me were doing the same thing. I sat down again, a little chilly and aware that I was blushing, something I hadn't done in years. So were a lot of other people. I was suppressing laughter, but it wasn't a nervous or joking laughter. It was amazement that here I was, in a room of thirty or thirty-five other men, all of them probably aware (as I was) of every imperfection in their own bodies, every little secret that they had trained themselves for years to hide because they were afraid they wouldn't be attractive to other men, or to the world in general.

There was still a lot of arguing going on. Some people protested that they weren't interested in an orgy, although we looked less like an orgy than most social gatherings I have

seen. In fact, we looked somewhat like a rather bewildered
gym class in a school for aging, freaky, bright children. It was
very hard for me to get upset about it. The only shadow that
crossed my mind was a question that had puzzled me in
adolescence, when I first heard of nudist camps. If a man is
in a situation with a lot of sexually desirable people, what's
going to happen if he shows any natural inclinations? I was
a little worried about that. Looking around, I saw other
people looking determinedly straight ahead at nothing, trying
to be very open and yet scared to death that they would give
something away. But it never happened, at least to anyone
I saw. It really was like a gym class; as the evening progressed,
I felt more relaxed, less self-conscious, more *innocent* than
I ever had in a straight locker room at school.

The whole thing seemed so funny, and so strange, that it
was impossible to keep looking at our situation as a meeting.
If the first man who removed his clothes had wanted to shock
us out of our routine, he had certainly succeeded. I started
talking to the people around me, only one of whom still had
his clothes on. Nobody badgered him; rather, we tried to
figure out why some of us had so readily stripped while others
obdurately refused to do so. I tried to explain how I felt like
responding to the man's personal appeal, which I felt was a
sincere, perhaps even overemotional, but valid and necessary
attempt to reach other people, to do something besides talk
or listen to talk. Another man said that he did it just to see
what it felt like. Still another said that he did it because
everyone else seemed to be doing it and honestly admitted that
his principal motive was the need for inconspicuousness.

A young man next to me, whom none of us had seen
before, said that he was afraid, before he did it, that other
people would find his body ugly, and that no one would like
him. I later learned that he was a teacher in a small Roman
Catholic college in New Jersey; he had summoned up all his
courage to come to this meeting because he wanted to meet

some people, to find out that he was not alone in his dilemma —and he did view his life as a homosexual teacher as a genuine dilemma. He was a handsome man; it was unlikely that most people could find fault with any part of his physical appearance. But he had learned to distrust and be ashamed of the sexual nature of his body, like a good American boy, and he had the added burden of shame inherent in being a homosexual. And I realized that I had had those feelings too, that I had wondered as I slipped off my jeans how I was going to look to these other men. But I had gone ahead and done it, as he had; once we were naked, we had no choice but to stop worrying about how we looked.

There was still a lot of sniggering going on; maybe this was finally going to be the orgy that everyone outside the movement envisioned as our daily routine. But the camp-counselor types among us (I have never been in a group of more than four people where there was not a camp counselor) took over, and we quickly fell into groups for games. A few people protested, but no one tried to coerce them into joining; that was exactly what we were trying to avoid. I had seen people in Central Park playing these games on weekends; they were mixed groups of men and women, and most of them seemed to be strangers to each other. I had always felt extremely embarrassed at the idea of joining them; now it seemed perfectly natural. We formed a circle, with one person in the middle; he then relaxed completely, falling forward or whichever way his body leaned. People caught him, gently, and then easily passed him around the circle, with the slightest bit of pressure, from man to man. The sensation was unique; totally physical, yet not in the least specifically sexual. There was another exercise in which a large group of people picked up one man and collectively supported him above their heads with the palms of their hands, then passing him around in various directions.

I remember thinking at one point how ridiculous we would

look to an outsider. But there weren't any outsiders; it was impossible that there could *be* any outsiders, because no one would be there unless he wanted to be. After an hour or so, people started getting dressed and leaving; others stayed on to talk, some for hours. I came away feeling that somehow I had accomplished something, certainly something more important than taking off my clothes and playing games. Someone had made an appeal to me as a homosexual, and I had answered that appeal by taking action. I had learned something about the way my self-image worked, and I had some real contact with other people, too. And I had had a good time, with no worries about what it all meant, or was I being taken for a ride, or how would I feel about it in the morning. It was another new experience, which made me optimistic—for the first time, I realized—about myself and all homosexuals as functioning individuals, not just victims of oppression.

• • •

In September, 1970, I gradually stopped going to meetings of the Gay Liberation Front. I had been attending regularly since May, and I finally, and reluctantly, realized that attendance had reached the point of diminishing returns. I agreed with the aims of the group, but I felt that it had a much more politically radical stance than I personally could reach. I had learned a great deal about myself, about homosexuality, and about the state of this country at those meetings. But I felt I had reached an impasse. I seemed to be seeing and hearing the same things over and over again. We talked and talked and talked about oppression, but that didn't change the fact of genuine oppression in my life. The GLF was talking about destroying society; I had my hands full worrying about the attitudes of my family and friends. The GLF was extremely concerned, and rightly so, with drawing up a position paper that would show exactly where it stood on all the important issues—sexism, racism, economic subjection of others, age chauvinism, and so on; I was worried, in a more mundane but equally urgent manner, about how I would meet that month's rent.

As I became more involved in the issues and implications of the gay liberation movement, my life changed drastically. *Time* magazine would probably say that I had dropped out, but I felt that I was simply reaching a more realistic perspective about what I wanted from my life. The first thing to go was my job; I had been feeling restive for months before I had even thought about gay liberation, and every day that I attempted to keep to the 9-to-5 routine made me even more tense. I had started planning to write this book and sketched about thirty pages, when I finally gave notice. Looking back, I see it was a foolhardy move but one I have never regretted. It is difficult to portray the incredibly wide-ranging and pervasive hold that heterosexuality has on the business and social life of the middle class in this country. As I listened to the GLF at nights and on weekends, I realized that my days were suffocating me.

Suddenly, daily conversations that I had once enjoyed or ignored became tedious and even offensive. Every anecdote about the little lovers' spats that people in the office had with their mates, every amusing story about what someone's child had said the night before, every excited account of a heavy date a secretary had gone through, every sly or innocent question about how long was I going to be a bachelor or how were my girlfriends or wasn't it time I settled down with a good woman—all were suddenly more than a sign of other people's interest or concern. They were a pain in the ass. They were unknowing, but extremely painful, attempts to fit me into the heterosexual scheme of things. I didn't *look* like a faggot, so I could therefore be straight. Or at least keep my mouth shut if I was otherwise.

When I finally stopped working in an office, an enormous weight was lifted from my shoulders. Most of the people there knew by then I was gay, because luckily I was publishing this book with the company I had worked for. It gave me an excuse to talk to some of them before leaving about the things that had bothered me. But I felt that they could not begin to understand what the gay liberation movement was about or that my growing alienation from the Gay Liberation Front in no way affected my wary suspicions about the straight world.

I also changed my living situation: I moved from a small apartment I had kept by myself in an expensive residential district into a loft east of Greenwich Village, which was situated in a sort of nest of painters and writers. Here I had to do everything myself—carpentry, plumbing, flooring. I let my hair grow. I started doing free-lance work at home. I got a puppy, which immediately started growing into a big shaggy dog. In short, I opted out of most of my old responsibilities and very cautiously assumed a few new ones.

On a more personal—and much more tentative—level, I had become involved in an emotional and sexual relationship with another man. This provided me with a concrete area for change. If I believed all the stuff I was ingesting at GLF meetings, this was the place to prove it. He was also deeply involved with the concepts of gay liberation, although he had been turned off to meetings and organized groups just as I was getting into them. We met at a GLF dance, but I quickly found out that he was even more wary than I of the implications of mass movements. As the relationship deepened, I was surprised and relieved to find out that it could all be reconciled—that the politics of sex could be risen above, that you could realize the damage being done to homosexuals and still have a positive relationship yourself, that such a relationship could even deepen your commitment to changing the world surrounding the two of you.

But I also realized that many of my expectations had changed or disappeared. As much as I valued this relationship, I could not make it the focus of my life. I could not abandon my individuality and my need for expression in order to pursue "love." This need for someone else to make one's life worthwhile was a useless notion fostered by the straight world. I could certainly live without Jim, and would if I wanted to do so. We came to each other freely, with no obligations, and I found myself thus much more deeply involved than I had ever been before. To try to put all my abstract generalizations into practice was hard; because we were in a relationship did not mean that we owned one another, and the conflicts were, and are, intense. But, when it worked, we had something that was not a parody of straight married life, nor a retreat from the challenges of homosexuality. It was simply what it was, and that turned out to be something very deep and good.

• • •

While I was making these radical personal adjustments, I was reaching the saturation point with radical politics. In my first flush of enthusiasm, I had tried to accept the GLF and everything it stood for. I was now beginning to realize I still had to take care of myself, to make sure that I wouldn't be swamped by the city, as I saw so many others were. I was tired of listening to other people, tired of hearing the same charges and countercharges. I had definitely committed myself to doing this book, and I began to feel that I would have to make my contribution to the movement that way. I mentioned the book to several people in the GLF; each wondered if I could perhaps make it a collective effort, so that it would not express just the biases of one man. I thought about this and realized that I wasn't, at least at this point, capable of working that closely with any group of people. I got a part-time job to support myself, tried to work on the book as often as possible, and proceeded to drop out of the gay liberation movement as well as the straight life.

But being a homosexual is a full-time condition, like being a woman or being a black. I remained extremely interested in what the GLF was doing, and I kept running into people who were still active. I also was interested in joining a new consciousness-raising group, one that I could be sure was more stable and personally productive than the last. After a few false starts, several people had tentatively decided to join the group. One of these, a young teacher, also expressed interest in getting involved in one of the gay activist organizations. Since my principal experience had been with the GLF, we decided to go to a GLF meeting, where he could see what went on for himself, and I could see how the group I had known had developed.

A gay community center—the ultimate goal for many of the original GLF people—had finally been obtained. Most of the financial backing came from GLF members, as did most of the people who worked there; I had heard about this from a member of my old consciousness-raising group. He had devoted an enormous amount of time and energy working for this community center and had been extremely optimistic about its prospects. I was anxious to see what he and his co-workers had accomplished. I felt somewhat guilty about my inability to keep working with the GLF, and perhaps this kind of atmosphere was what I needed to get me going again.

My friend and I had an unpleasant surprise. All the bad things that I remembered about the GLF seemed multiplied, intensified, and most of the good things seemed to be gone. I was supposed to meet him there; I was a little late, and, when I arrived, I saw no sign of him at first. I said hello to one man whom I recognized, and I tried to take in the scene. There were several people wandering about, and several people sleeping; several transvestites were there, but no women. I learned that there was a separate women's caucus going on at the same time. The transvestites were engaged in a violent argument, with much whispering in corners and shouting across the room. There were several people who looked suspiciously like junkies or pushers. (Even in the most liberal and most radical circles in New York, the unknown junkie is the one person who is always feared. Most people have one or two friends who are junkies, but those who are unknown are feared and often hated. They are the ones who rob you, no matter how poor you may be, and they are the ones who sometimes even kill.)

I saw my friend then; he was slumped on a couch, hunched up in his duffle coat and looking around with a half-frightened, half-disappointed air. I went over and joined him, trying to explain that he wasn't really seeing the whole picture, that things were often quite different. He stared at me doubtfully. I suppose I didn't sound very convincing, probably because I didn't believe half of what I was saying myself. He wanted to go immediately, but I persuaded him to stay and see what would happen. Which turned out to be nothing.

The gay community center is situated on the second floor of a four-story building, which houses one of the original folk-singing hangouts. The building is located in the middle of a garish, pathetic cluster of clubs, "art" galleries, pizza parlors, and ice cream stands, which are thronged with tourists and teen-agers every weekend. There is a resident community that exists among, but completely independent of, the mobs of the curious. It is part of this community that established and runs the center. When I was going to the center that night, I must admit that I got a certain amount of pleasure, an almost elitist little thrill at the thought that I was part of the underground, that I was going to a place completely unknown to most of the people around me. When we got there, the actuality of what I was seeing dispelled my fantasies.

The center is one large room, with many small rooms created by partitions in odd places for the use of various groups within the gay community. The women have a special room of their own, where they hold their own meetings and remain independent of the male dominance that so doggedly insists on surfacing in what would seem to be the most radical group imaginable. The other spaces are used by the Third World Gay Liberation Front, the Gay Youth group, political education caucuses, and the like. The plan of the space was very ambitious, but, like so many parts of the gay liberation movement, the aims and possibilities of the plan far outstripped the actual execution. Everything looked as though it had been attempted and then abandoned —painting, building, artwork.

Everyone seemed tired and discouraged, and the amount of open hostility far exceeded anything I had ever witnessed in the movement. Instead of being a minority within the group, that night the transvestites seemed to dominate. They, in turn, appeared to be controlled by the hoods who were also hanging around. I had heard that there were a lot of suspicious-looking characters at the center, and my informant also gave me his personal opinion: "I think a lot of them aren't even gay." I agreed with him. It was discouraging and frightening; it seemed that an important and promising part of the gay movement was being taken over and destroyed, just for the hell of it, not even for reasons of ideological conflict. Nobody could ever victimize the Weathermen or the women's lib groups or even the Black Panthers to that extent. Homosexuals had been cast in the role of victims for centuries, and I wondered if a lot of us could ever break out of that role.

My friend and I left without waiting for the meeting (if it ever took place). He was deeply shaken. He had wanted to do something, to get out of a rut of going to gay bars, being bored there, and yet being unable to express his homosexuality in any other way. But this was too much. He had even less in common with these people than he did with people in the bars. I had nothing to reassure him with. I was even more disturbed. I had devoted a lot of time to GLF and then let up to pursue my personal interests. Was this the result of a lot of people doing the same thing or was it intrinsic in the nature of any such group to dissolve in chaos? I was a little frightened of finding out the answer to that one, but I determined that I would have to go back and find out.

We formed a new group, one that I think functioned much more successfully than my previous group had. The work, both physical and psychological, that this entailed was exhausting, but the benefits it produced were enormous. This activity, combined with my work on the book, meant that I was regularly devoting a major portion of my life to the study of homosexuality, both that of myself and that of others. I thought, with some trepidation, about returning to the GLF meetings. I really didn't want to be disappointed again, especially when the projects I was doing myself seemed to be working. But curiosity and the old Protestant duty that had to see everything to its logical conclusion won out, and I went back again to see what was going on.

• • •

My next few visits to the GLF both reassured and disturbed me. Things seemed to have balanced out once again, and yet this only confirmed the impossibility of ever really knowing where one stood. The next meeting I attended was in March, 1971, almost a year after that first momentous encounter. A lot had changed. The gay community center became the Gay Liberation Front Center at that meeting, since it was funded by GLF money and staffed by GLF people. But the major change was in the actual appearance of the place. I had heard, once again through the grapevine, that there had been some sort of tightening up, and it showed. There were no more hoods hanging around, which immediately set me at ease. There was a lot of fresh paint on the walls; in fact, all through the meeting a woman was perched on top of a tall ladder, painting an enormous wall very carefully with a small brush. Somehow, that was very affecting. There were new posters up and a large bulletin board that was either new or that I hadn't noticed on my one previous visit. There weren't many people there, only twenty or so when the meeting started and about thirty-five by the time I left. But the meeting started roughly on time, which was a first in my acquaintance with the GLF. Things had changed a lot.

There was still a chairman chosen by lot, but there was a new structure for making decisions. Items were still discussed according to consensus, until all who wanted to could speak about what they thought to be relevant. Now, however, voting was being used, not as any attempt at "democracy" (which I had already realized was a virtually impossible method for achieving our aims), but for the sake of expediency. There was a lot of business on the agenda, all of it very specific and most of it quickly handled. Discussions of demonstrations alternated with appeals for money and announcements of services and items for sale that were available from people in the movement. One man showed T-shirts, available from the Peace Parade Committee, adorned with a likeness of Mme. Nguyen Thi Binh, the woman who heads North Vietnam's delegation to the Paris peace talks, above which was the caption "Live Like Her." He spoke briefly about how it was rumored that she might be gay but that at any rate she and the Peace Committee deserved our support.

Several plans for large coordinated demonstrations were proposed and discussed, as well as an announcement of plans for a trip to Albany that weekend with gay activist groups of all political persuasions to demonstrate before legislators who were about to discuss repealing antihomosexual laws in New York state. This solidarity struck me; it was the strongest cooperation I had seen between the GLF and other groups on a specific, planned action, and it was being handled as a matter of course. There was also a union representative, who talked about a gay caucus that was recently formed in his local; he asked for people to come and talk with the union, and for permission to have union speakers address the GLF. There was initial hostility to what some (including myself) saw as an incursion by an established tool of the establishment—labor unions—into such an avowedly radical group, but his obvious sincerity carried him as he attempted to show how people who *had* to work within the system still had to be helped and how it could be done.

I finally left during this discussion. I was interested, but I was also tired, and the future of the GLF and the productivity of this meeting certainly did not hinge on my presence. I thought about the meeting for days afterward and periodically returned to meetings in the next few months to confirm what I had decided. I was with the GLF, and, more importantly, it was with me. It wasn't a matter of who belonged to what, but rather a whole state of mind, a radicalization of one's entire being, that was the issue.

Recent events have strengthened this feeling. The GLF has gone through yet another procedural change. It has formalized its membership requirements, asking that members be in either a consciousness-raising group or a political education group for at least a month before attending members' meetings. These meetings are held separately from larger forums for the whole gay community, which have replaced the old Sunday night meetings and which are general discussions on any current topics of interest to the radical gay community. This formalization depressed me, but, at the same time, I realized it was probably inevitable if the GLF wished to continue to be an effective force.

The success or failure of any individual or group of individuals was important, but not nearly as significant as the fact that there was a movement, a change in the thinking of our culture that had been started and would not stop until it had fully developed. People like myself could agonize all we wanted about levels of commitment and purity of ideology, but we were still involved in that change. And it was irreversible. In the largest sense, it is impossible to drop out of the homosexual liberation movement. Once you are there, you are there for good. I had intellectually believed in it from the beginning, but now I had reached the point where intellectual decisions were no longer necessary. I was living a revolution.

6 *other ways*

LIKE MOST MOVEMENTS and groups in America, gay liberation has a left, a center, and a right. My sympathies on most issues are with the left, and this is no exception. But, just as I feel slightly guilty about not being able to be a twenty-four-hour textbook revolutionary, I feel obligated to discuss the other, more traditional elements within the movement.

I had first become acquainted with the Gay Activists' Alliance at the same time I started thinking about the GLF. Both groups ran ads in the *Voice* and had been described in articles I had read. The GLF was described as radical, while the GAA was supposed to be more concerned with the single issue of homosexual rights. I didn't quite get the distinction, but it seemed that the GAA people would probably be somehow ... nicer.

I went to a GAA meeting before I attended any GLF meetings or dances. That first meeting remains rather vague in my mind; I went for the same reasons that a few weeks later drew me to the GLF, but I remember none of the nervousness I later felt. The GAA meets in the same room in the same church as the GLF did when I first encountered it. But, when I walked into the room that night, I felt no surprise at what I saw. There were about seventy-five people there, and they seemed to be a representative sample of white, middle-class, male homosexuals. I don't think there was anybody there with whom I could not have carried on a comfortable conversation about mutual interests—if I could loosen up enough to talk with anyone at all.

But several people went out of their way to make me welcome, asking me my name, if it was my first time here, and so on. Evidently there was some sort of semiofficial greeting committee. Just like at college mixers, I thought skeptically. I read a little flyer as I waited for the meeting to begin; it stated the requirements for joining the GAA. "In order to become a member of GAA, you must attend three general meetings within a six-week period, one meeting of any committee, and one orientation session. After fulfilling these requirements, you become a member on payment to the membership secretary of an entrance fee of one dollar. Members are expected to remain active on a steady basis in at least one committee."

This scared me: I had hardly ever gone to gay bars because I was nervous in the company of a lot of homosexuals. Now I had to sign statements and commit myself to attending meetings and be on committees. All I wanted to do was be a little happier when I made out, but this was like joining the Young Democrats. So I kept quiet and tried to stay as uninvolved as possible. Looking around the room, I noticed there were four or five people like myself, trying to appear on top of it and yet blend into the woodwork at the same time.

There was only one woman. Except for the newcomers, everyone seemed to be having a good time.

The meeting progressed quite evenly. The officers assembled around a table and introduced themselves. Someone gave a précis on what the GAA was all about, and then came reports from various committees. There was evidently a very strict procedure, with formal rules of order, and it was very carefully followed. No one spoke out of turn, and every issue was voted on by a show of hands from qualified members. There were several references to GAA-GLF hostility, which I didn't understand; after all, they were all homosexuals, so where could the conflict lie, except in some sort of petty power struggle?

I don't remember the topics that were talked about that evening, nor do I remember the outcome of any of the discussions. I do remember being very bored. I knew everyone was talking about important issues—ideas I was just beginning to appreciate about how homosexuals were made to function in society. But I wasn't moved. Nobody said anything that made me want to do anything myself, to change anything about the way I lived. The formality and strict conduct of the meeting bothered me. I knew they were probably necessary if anything was to be accomplished, but they still seemed so strict that I felt I probably wouldn't be able to function with the group. I didn't know anybody there, and, although several people were very friendly, I had no one with whom to compare viewpoints or even make a few jokes. (This, I have come to believe, is crucial in forming an organization of homosexuals, perhaps of any group. Very few people can come in off the street and stay interested for very long. People have to be very close to at least a few other people from the beginning, or cohesion will be very difficult. That is why consciousness-raising groups seem to be an ideal way for people to first encounter gay liberation.)

But what disturbed me most about the GAA was its

general orientation. The Gay Activists' Alliance makes very clear that it is basically a one-issue group. It is not interested in supporting or getting involved with other struggles—for example, those of blacks, Puerto Ricans, women—reasoning that homosexuals have enough to worry about just making sure that they get what is coming to them. Moreover, the group as thus defined could represent the entire spectrum of the gay community, from left-wingers to rabidly conservative (the surprisingly large number of politically right-wing homosexuals has always puzzled and disappointed me) .

All my experiences before I encountered the gay liberation movement, and everything that has happened to me since, have convinced me that homosexuality as a life style cannot be separated from the world it exists in. Homosexuality is a political state, just as being black or being a woman is a political state. We are not trained to think that way, yet we *are* forced into certain economic, social, and cultural roles that are virtually inescapable until we identify ourselves as belonging to a political group. If we don't recognize that the entire system is geared to keeping people in these sexual or racial roles, with escape limited to a few—whether Gore Vidal or Ralph Bunche or Margaret Chase Smith—then we will never really change what is oppressing us.

I hadn't articulated all this, of course, when I went to that GAA meeting, but I do remember being vaguely disappointed at what I felt to be the limited scope of the organization's viewpoint. They were worried about job security, but I had never experienced any opposition on a job—because I could easily pass as straight, I later realized. They were worried about police harassment, whereas I was very careful to avoid any situation where the police would have occasion to harass me—I later realized that *all* police are trained to view *all* public acknowledgment of homosexuality as suspicious and all physical homosexual acts as criminal. They were involved with the mundane things that I had stopped worrying about years ago. I could take these problems seriously when they were part of discrimination against blacks or Puerto Ricans or Jews, but it would take a group like GLF to jolt me into realizing that these concerns were *my* concerns, that I couldn't simply opt for comfort when other people were suffering for what I chose to forget.

I still have not related personally to what the GAA is doing; it has been by far the most publicity conscious of all homosexual groups and, as such, has made great progress. Homosexuality is acknowledged as an existing way of life now in places where it was previously ignored, such as television, the *New York Times*, Governor Rockefeller's office. The GAA seemed to be doing fine without me, which is great; every homosexual who takes a step toward liberation does it for everyone else. But I would not be honest if I didn't admit that I disagreed with some of its stances. Many of its leading members seem to work quite hard at becoming media personalities. Their pictures appear weekly in gay periodicals; they are quoted at length by straight reporters; they work at being spokesmen for the entire gay community. Yet their rigid disapproval of any political stand by their organization other than on purely "homosexual issues" seems to make it impossible for them to represent many people like myself, who feel that homosexual oppression is part of a larger malady inherent in our society.

I became involved in the Gay Liberation Front rather than the GAA for reasons that I did not understand then and that I don't fully understand now. But, in the comfortable routine that I had set up for myself before the GLF, I felt a dissatisfaction, which I didn't feel the GAA's solutions would alleviate. Although their issues were certainly genuine, what would be the change once all their reforms were accomplished? Would I be happier in a world where no one was fired from a job in advertising or the military establishment because he was homosexual? Would I be happier if I knew the police would not raid a bar, so I could stand around with a beer in my hand for hours, eying other people doing the same thing? Would I be happier if gay people had all the same privileges *and* boring preoccupations as happily married straight couples? Racism, sexism, the military-industrial complex—all these things *do* exist. They are not only not separate from the oppression of homosexuals, they also compound the dilemmas of millions of homosexuals. Although I certainly admire and respect what the GAA has done, I feel that, until it confronts these problems, it will be part of the liberal syndrome of reform and compromise that always lets us half solve our problems and then ends up frustrating us to the point of apathy.

·   ·   ·

The Mattachine Society is the oldest homosexual group in the country. Founded fifteen years ago, it was until recently the only formal organization attempting to work with the problems of homosexuals. I remember reading about the Mattachine Society when I was a child, probably about the time that I first heard the word homosexual. The Mattachine Society is widely viewed by young, radical homosexuals as the NAACP of the homosexual movement. But, like the NAACP, it has done very important things; its groundwork is one of the most important bases for today's homosexual activists. When Mattachine members first spoke out, the climate of this country was much more repressive than it is today. It took a great deal of courage to do what they did, as much as any radical today possesses.

But the same passage of time, which has created a generation gap between the radical left of the 1930's and today's SDS, Weathermen, and Progressive Labor Party, has left the Mattachine with a heritage of demonstrations and campaigns that now seem cautious and narrow in scope. Just as people in the GLF deride the GAA, people in the GAA think of the Mattachine as a rusty anachronism, and the process also works the other way. Despite the fact that we are all in this together, there is much hostility, both direct and sublimated, among the various groups. The two focuses of the Mattachine—homosexual rights and personal counseling—are dwarfed compared to the massive law-changing public relations effort of the GAA and the commitment of the GLF to change all of Western society. But, once again, what would seem to be true and what actually happens turn out to be very different, certainly much more different from anything I had expected.

The Mattachine Society no longer holds meetings. It has several thousand dues-paying members, and the whole meeting structure evidently became very unwieldy. It has an office on West End Avenue in New York, where the local branch has it headquarters; this is where it carries out its extensive counseling functions. It also sponsors actions that it encourages its members to support and provides various social services for homosexuals as well as an extensive library on every aspect of homosexuality.

I first went there on a Saturday afternoon. I was not particularly eager to go, but I figured it was only fair to present all sides of the homosexual movement. The small office, located in an old but well-kept-up apartment building, was nearly empty when I entered. There was one visitor, an older man of about sixty and a young staff member of about twenty-five. The older man left after a few minutes, and I explained to the young man, whose name was Warren, that I was doing a book on gay liberation, concentrating on the impact of the GLF, and that I also wanted to try to show what was going on in other groups, such as the Mattachine.

We talked for an hour or so; during that time I gradually altered my whole concept of what the Mattachine was trying

to do. The other groups and individuals I had seen and
talked with were clearly convinced that homosexuals had to
fight against oppression. In the Mattachine, the emphasis
was on helping individuals adjust to being gay. Its political
stance, always cautious and tentative, seemed to have
withered away. But its role as dispenser of advice and counseling was thriving. While I was there, the phone must have
rung twenty times, with people inquiring about matters
ranging from the upcoming demonstration in Albany to a
list of good gay bars for a newcomer in town.

Warren was obviously willing to talk with me about every
aspect of the Mattachine's operations. I mentioned the image
that Mattachine had acquired as an older, conservative,
almost stodgy group, and he told me how much that had
led to that characterization had changed since a group of
younger men had started taking a very active role in the organization. He explained that Mattachine saw itself as basically
an agency for help, and he gave me several pamphlets. One
dealt with VD, how to know if you have it and what to do;
another gave detailed instructions on what to do in case of
arrest; a third examined practical problems of the homosexual in the armed forces. We also discussed the other
groups I had seen. He was very complimentary about their
activities, carefully noting that the Mattachine did not feel
that these were in its province but that it certainly supported
everything other groups were doing. I found this difficult to
accept totally, because the GLF, at least, seemed committed
to destroying many things that Mattachine people still deeply
believed in—for example, the male role and the concept of
economic advancement within the capitalist system. Warren
said that there were areas where agreement was not total but
that all homosexuals were working for the same basic free-
doms. I wondered.

He told me about how crowded the office was on weekday
nights, when out-of-town people arrived to learn about gay

life in the city, students and researchers came in to use the library, men who were just coming out of the closet ventured in to acknowledge themselves as homosexual for the first time. I asked about women in the group; he said that Mattachine had originally had many women members and that they had eventually left to found their own organization, the Daughters of Bilitis. There were still women on the Mattachine mailing list, however. As we were talking about this, a woman entered; she stayed for half an hour, talking freely about her life as a lesbian married to a straight man. Warren was just as interested in everything she had to say as he seemed to be in my conversation. I was becoming impressed with his tact and skill in handling the role of listener. Even though the woman, who was there to meet a woman friend, would almost certainly never be active in the Mattachine Society, he was giving her as much attention as he would give a long-standing male worker in the Mattachine.

Soon after she left, the phone rang, and Warren became very involved with the caller. Since the office was quite small, I couldn't help overhearing what he was saying. After he had talked about fifteen minutes, he hung up; he verified what I had gathered from hearing his end of the conversation. A man, evidently near hysteria, had called from some western state. He was a prominent administrator at a state university and had been arrested by the police while performing a sexual act with a student in a public place. He pleaded guilty and was fired. His arrest was public knowledge. All this came out in the course of the conversation. Warren's first advice was to move to a big city and try to live in the homosexual life style he seemed to desire. The man then told him about his family—he was married and the father of several children. This complicated matters enormously, because the Mattachine, like most gay organizations, deals primarily with single homosexuals. Warren referred him to the nearest homophile group in his area and gave him some pertinent advice on dealing with lawyers and with the charges that were being processed against him. The whole situation gave me pause. A man in such trouble would never have called the GLF, nor, in all probability, would he have contacted the GAA. Yet there are hundreds of thousands of homosexuals who get into serious trouble, and somebody has to deal with their problems. The Mattachine Society had not moved into the arena of sweeping social changes. It was simply trying to help people cope. I certainly would not have been able to help that man; the Mattachine had much to offer him.

As we concluded our talk, Warren continued to be completely even-handed. I was uncomfortable with the situation of the woman who had visited the office and the man who had called in such distress. They were not free agents, they had to deal with families and faculties and arrest records, all the impediments that we self-styled revolutionaries simply skipped around. It was reassuring to know that there was someone who could give these people more than radical rhetoric.

When I got home and looked over the Mattachine newsletters, my doubts resurfaced. There were numerous references to left-wing homosexuals who kept bewailing their "imaginary" oppression. That was supposed to be me, I guessed. The services offered—gay pen-pal clubs, a reliable guide to mail-order physique photo dealers, solutions to conflicts between religion and sexual desire, guides to gay bars and hotels abroad—all seemed so hollow, so redolent of *The Boys in the Band*, which was one of the newsletter's ten best films of the year. The newsletters also shared the preoccupation with printing anything that had anything to do with homosexuality, which seems to be common in all gay newspapers outside the radical left. The Mattachine pamphlets proudly stated that it had forced the New York State Liquor Authority to recognize the legality of gay bars and to stop police harassment on Fire Island. These seemed to me dubious achievements, victories that simply perpetuated the cycle of ghettos and insularity that has kept the gay world from confronting the straight world.

But there was still the young man listening patiently in that office to a classic closet case who had been caught. He was dealing with homosexual oppression at least as much as I was, in his own way. There may be a generation gap between older and younger homosexuals, but he was right in believing that we are all in this together. I might easily be arrested someday; Warren might come to see the basic inequities of American capitalism. Whatever happens, we are all going to be queers and perverts in the public mind for many years. However we attack that characterization, we will be working together, whether our ideologies jibe to our satisfaction or not.

• • •

In May, 1971, I went to the opening dance at the Gay Activists' Alliance's new community center in the lower Village—an old firehouse the GAA had taken over, with all four floors being used for its activities. By GAA standards, the dance was enormously successful: over a thousand people attended and there were only three summonses. Admission was inexpensive; beer and soda were only a quarter. There were hundreds of interesting, attractive people meeting hundreds of other interesting, attractive people. But all my reservations about the group were brought out there, for the very same reasons that the GAA was overjoyed. I couldn't see much difference between this and an enormous, all-male singles bar. Of course, I was glad that the Mafia wasn't getting our money. But many of my anxieties about gay bars were only increased here. There were perhaps fifty men there that I would have liked to relate to. Which one should I pick? And would they want to relate to me? Suppose they could do better, or I could do better? Despite all our talk of liberation, this dance didn't seem to be too far from where I had started.

A meeting of my consciousness-raising group was scheduled for the next day, and I found myself anticipating it eagerly, as I surveyed the crowded dance floor with what I hoped was a blasé gaze. I suddenly felt very warm toward all the people in my group. I could tell them about all my reservations concerning the dance, and they would understand—not because they were unusually intelligent or sensitive, but because we were close to one another. They were what I really needed—not this dance, even though I could enjoy myself this evening.

Walking home that night, still feeling good about my group, I had another insight. There wouldn't be any group if it weren't for dances like these and the organizations that sponsored them. And I wouldn't be involved in the relationship that was giving me such extraordinary pleasure. It didn't matter that I didn't have great revelations about every gay movement dance I went to; they were still very important and useful events. My life and their work could certainly co-exist.

• • •

Perhaps I will be accused of slighting those homosexual groups that prefer to work "within the system." I truly do not mean to. I simply want to communicate my simultaneous confusion and optimism over the complexity in the homosexual world. I have until recently unconsciously shared the assumptions of numerous researchers, all straight people, and many homosexuals that homosexuality is still a shadow world, a sort of cloudy mirror image of straight life that must be protected and nurtured. It is not. These groups will almost certainly thrive without my help or even with my opposition. They are far healthier than comparable groups in the straight world. Perhaps that is because homosexuals have always, no matter what their economic or social status, had to work very hard to keep functioning at all. Consequently, most of us are very strong people. Our lives and culture, though they have been ignored for centuries, thrive; that is why the straight world continues to view us as a threat. I, as an individual, will continue to dispute points with the Gay Activists' Alliance and with the Mattachine Society. The individuals in those groups will respond, and most likely one side or the other will eventually win its point. But neither side will go under. There will be some sort of unity. We *are* all queers.

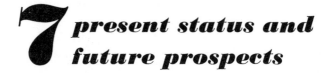

7 present status and future prospects

THE GAY LIBERATION movement, as a phenomenon that can potentially affect *all* homosexuals, is in its infancy. Scarcely two and one-half years ago, the riots at the Stonewall Inn signaled the beginning, but the implications have grown continually and are constantly being discovered, rediscovered, and explored, by homosexuals, by the media, and even by the fearful and moribund straight world.

The months between my decision to undertake this book and its completion have been filled with incidents that show the scope and impact of this revolution—for it must be called a revolution, in the truest sense of the word. The first, and most concrete, area of change was in the activities of organizations—the Gay Liberation Front, the Gay Activists' Alliance, the Daughters of Bilitis, the Mattachine Society, Homosexuals Intransigent, and many others in the New York City area; their achievements are of course paralleled and their impact is multiplied by the work of similar organizations in every major city and on college campuses throughout the nation.

The second, perhaps most visible, chain of developments has started in the media. From viewing homosexuality as a subject of derision at best, to be treated as a sort of aberrant cross between child molestation and Fire Island caricatures, radio, television, and particularly newspapers have finally decided to try to portray homosexuals as homosexuals. They have begun considering homosexuality as something other than a crime topic hidden at the bottom of the back pages of newspapers or the subject of novels whose authors' sexual preferences are politely overlooked.

The third wave of change—the least visible to the outsider, and, to me at least, by far the most profound—is the cumulative self-realization and subsequent changes in life styles that are affecting hundreds of thousands, perhaps millions, all over the country. Their personal crises, soulsearching, and difficult decisions are rarely described. Many times, they are scarcely able themselves to articulate the turmoil through which they are passing. But it is here that the homosexual revolution has its greatest effect, because it is in peoples' lives that all movements are ultimately tested. The implications of homosexuality are of course inextricably bound up with the sexual act; but they also reach into every other area of our lives—social, cultural, economic, and political.

The Gay Activists' Alliance has steadily covered ground in the civil rights fight. The group's most visible manifestations are demonstrations, which are often stagy, even a little pretentious to those who judge such matters aesthetically. But they serve their purposes well—confronting John Lindsay and Thomas Hoving, outside a Metropolitan Museum opening, over homosexuals in city government; cheerfully raiding a series of offices of the Household Finance Corporation, demanding that investigations of homosexuals' private lives be stopped; sitting in at Nelson Rockefeller's office to demand that antihomosexual laws be repealed. The GAA's efforts have begun to bring results. It has demanded and received space on television and radio, including such bastions of enlightened liberal middle America as the Dick Cavett show. It has been the principal organizer of a drive that is now resulting in a serious attempt by the New York State legislature to amend laws forbidding homosexuality. Perhaps most important, it has persuaded politicians to speak out openly for homosexual rights. Notable among these is Bella Abzug, the highly vocal Manhattan Congresswoman whose clearly stated, though still cautious, support of GAA policies was a decisive factor in her election to Congress.

The Mattachine Society, struggling desperately to shore up its 1950's image, is right in there with the GAA, working for a better life for all homosexuals. It also stands by the Gay Liberation Front, although there is practically no communication between the two groups. The Mattachine role seems to have evolved into a support of all things homosexual, no matter what the motivation, source, or significance. Although this makes it perhaps ideologically irrelevant to those who view homosexuals as a potential force for revolution, the Mattachine's is a practical and useful approach. It provides information basics—what to do when arrested, how to handle the possibility of VD, where to find a good bar or Turkish bath. These are often important, even critical, problems, and they may even still be so after everybody has been liberated.

The Gay Liberation Front continues on its way—erratic, diffuse, the most imaginative and impractical of the activist groups and probably the one with the greatest potential for effecting genuine long-range change. For, despite my misgivings about the GLF, the direction it is going in could make the greatest difference in the conditions that have oppressed homosexuals for so long. It is the only group that is really integrated, both sexually and racially. It is the only group that is challenging the basic assumptions of American society, which continues to oppress most of its own people. It is the only group to experiment with new and radically different ways of living, especially in the communal area. Despite its need to certify itself as *truly* radical and revolutionary, the GLF is quintessentially the new homosexuality. Significantly, is has finally been able to start giving dances in its community center; at the same time, there are constant rumors about the center's imminent closing. That would be a tragedy. It is not simply that there is finally a place for radical homosexuals, those outside every part of the Establishment. For the center is also a gathering, a place of fusion for all kinds of gay people. It is in this way that the GLF occasionally reaches far beyond the passionate but easy pieties of radical rhetoric to show what people really can be.

The activities of these organizations have fostered several interesting events. Perhaps the most indicative was the drive for Congress by Franklin E. Kameny. Long familiar to old-line homosexual activists, Kameny gained new prominence as a candidate for Congress from the District of Columbia. Openly campaigning as a homosexual, Kameny was careful to declare that his candidacy represented all minority groups. Although he lost the election, the fact that he was able to get on the ballot at all is amazing. A few years ago, such a public declaration by anyone running for office would have been unthinkable. Today, it merits national press coverage, and not merely as a curiosity item. Busloads of gay activists descended on Washington to help collect signatures to place Kameny's name on the ballot. This wholesale cooperation is another significant factor. There is gradually arising a genuine cohesion among homosexuals, a sense of identity that can give them some force as a political entity in the American power structure. It is unlikely that candidates' consciences prompted them to come out for gay rights in the recent New York state elections. Rather, it was the realization that they were representing a state and city containing the largest concentration of homosexuals in the country, perhaps in the world, and that most of these people would vote. It was a strange and not altogether pleasant sight to see such liberals as Richard Ottinger, Charles Goodell, and Arthur Goldberg cautiously make their stands on the issues of sexual liberation.

Even more unexpected are the responses of religious organizations to homosexual demands. Troy Perry, a fundamentalist preacher in Los Angeles, has founded a church for homosexuals that has become the model for others all over the country. Perry, a slick revivalist who reminds at least one person (me) of the outdated menace of Elmer Gantry, is nevertheless filling a legitimate, even desperate, need of many homosexuals. His church is a place where they can be themselves, where, even if they are not religious, they can express the social side of homosexuality that is ignored by the straight world. And now the established churches are beginning to take note of the plight of the homosexual. Confronted by gay organizations and individuals, several churches have responded by forming commissions to study the problem, inviting speakers, pointing out past statements on the subject, and so on. Thus far, the Lutherans, Quakers, and Unitarians have made statements specifically supporting homosexual rights.

This interest by the churches is seen as pointless by most gay people. Older homosexuals who were raised in religious households are often still concerned about the attitude of the churches toward them, but, for more young activists, it is simply a matter of no concern. I personally feel more strongly about this. Being raised and educated as a Catholic,

I was subjected for years to the Church's antiphysical, morbidly moralistic world view. In this scheme, homosexuality was just another evil of the flesh, which didn't even have the validity that marriage gave to the deflowering of heterosexual male and female virgins. As I eventually realized that the Church itself contained an enormously sophisticated homosexual underworld of its own, I understood that all the preaching I had been subjected to, all the humiliating lectures on my abnormal desires that I had heard from priests in confessionals, were just one more example of the big coverup of a simple truth—that I could do whatever I wanted to, all by myself.

Thus, when I see churches beginning to reconsider their harsh judgments on homosexuality, I am resentful and often angered. After 2,000 years of Christianity's telling homosexuals they are unnatural, even evil, if they persist in their ways, the churches are finally giving us another chance. For what? To join them? The centuries of legislating morality are over, and hopefully all organized religions, the enforcers of that morality, will also fade away. But they must not expect homosexuals to keep them company in their death throes. The injustices and abuses they have heaped on homosexuals, whom they have victimized more than *any* other group, cannot be forgotten.

This about-face by our former oppressors frightens me when I look at the enormous range of operations being conducted by homophile groups. Where do we draw the line between the adjustment of social conditions and assimilation into the society that we are trying to change? In a sense, we are faced with the dilemma that has confronted all reformers: how can we keep from becoming that which we are reforming? The work of homosexual organizations is geared primarily toward changing laws; yet, when the laws are changed, as surely they will be, and all homosexual acts are legal, will our lives also be changed? Certainly, I don't disagree with anything the GAA or the Mattachine Society is trying to do, but I think that they are involved in a struggle where the ultimate issues are much more important than laws or legal sanctions or whether one can be employed by the U.S. Government. To solve all those (admittedly urgent) problems is not to eradicate the mystery of the homosexual.

Thus I find myself always drawn back to the Gay Liberation Front, not as an organization but as a force. What I have heard from people in the GLF has radicalized me, probably permanently. Despite my discomfort with many of its purely political stances, which seem doctrinaire and limited, I somehow feel that its almost anarchistic approach to our society, to sex, to our whole culture, is now the most viable one that I personally can deal with. We are all bearing the weight of 3,000 years of "civilization"; in this country, it has resulted in the Vietnam war, advertising, and network TV. It may have worked before, but it doesn't now. So perhaps the best thing to do is—once again—realize that we are all essentially alone, try to understand our past, pick out the best pieces, and start over again from scratch. We can't keep patching up an old machine that doesn't work anymore; that is what I feel most of the homophile groups are still doing. Only the GLF has faced the fact that homosexuals *as* homosexuals are and always have been outlaws and that it is impossible to turn around, shake hands, and join the game.

•   •   •

Homosexuals are still visible to most of the straight world through the media, primarily in newspapers and films and on television. Despite the fact that many suburban parents have a son or daughter who is homosexual, they will probably receive their information from their local newspaper's reports of sex crimes and psychiatrists' reports or from television, whose discussions of homosexuality range from the fair-minded but boring panels on educational TV to the sick and witless gibes of people like Bob Hope. It is sad that these people will get distorted or one-sided versions of gay life in these ways, rather than from their own children, but it is unfortunately true.

The fact that there even *was* a gay liberation movement first came to me through those oddly similar publications, the *Village Voice* and *Esquire*. After reading the *Voice*'s initial coverage of the Stonewall riots and subsequent gay demonstrations, I got the feeling that the *Voice* considered them a cross between the Saint Patrick's Day parade and those annual drag balls that used to delight the old tabloid photographers. But it was an article by Tom Burke in the August, 1969, *Esquire* that made the biggest impression on me. Accompanied by a totally irrelevant photograph of two Hell's Angels on a cycle with a "Just Married" sign who have been stopped by a cop, the article gave the lowdown on the new kind of homosexual in New York. Because I saw myself as the old kind of homosexual in New York, I was fascinated. I hadn't met anyone in my extensive travels around the city who resembled these charming, carefree creatures. Everyone in the article seemed cool, self-assured, beyond worries or cares in their new world. It was tempting; it certainly seemed to be a lot more fun than anything I was doing. The one exception to this mood was a young man who appeared briefly toward the end of the article; he was pictured berating an older straight man, a well-meaning liberal type, who, after the Christopher Street disturbances, wanted to know what these people wanted. The young man was furious, seemingly out of proportion to the incident; his reply was something like, "We want your children. I can have your daughter, but before that I'll screw your son." That scared and impressed me.

Much later, while I was preparing this book, an article appeared in the *New York Times* magazine. Of everything written about gay liberation thus far, this article seems to have had the greatest impact on the straight world. It has set off a chain of replies, attacks, and counterattacks that have catapulted gay liberation into a newsworthiness equal to black events, women's liberation, and new psychotherapeutic techniques. I read all these articles avidly and watched the reaction to them with great interest. Even though I felt myself to be in the process of becoming somehow personally radical, I had never seen these issues discussed this way. I had talked endless hours about gay liberation with people I knew, but I had never seen it blazoned across the pages of the good, grey *Times*.

The article that occasioned all this uproar was entitled "What It Means to Be a Homosexual." It was written by a novelist and former TV scriptwriter, Merle Miller. He is not a homosexual activist; he is a homosexual who has seen what these activists are doing and responded with his statement. It is a curious and ultimately depressing piece. Miller, who is about fifty, admits that he has been afraid until now to admit his homosexuality; and he shows how he was probably prudent to wait until now. The world wasn't ready for it, and neither was he. But now that he has made his public declaration, that persistent doubt appears again: is this it? Now what? I was glad that a homosexual could talk openly about homosexuality in a magazine that would reach millions of people who could learn from him. But I had to face the fact that his article, as courageous as it was, came from a consciousness that was trying to be indistinguishable from the standard liberal biases of the straight world.

I do not mean to put Miller down; but I believe he missed a great opportunity to show a real alternative to the straight society that is crippling so many people. Miller is a successful writer; he is a well-educated, appreciative man who evidently has led a full and rewarding life, marred (and I am not being ironic) by the hidden secret of his homosexuality. Now that he has taken the courageous—but not dangerous—step of admitting his homosexuality, he can turn to those straight friends of his and say, "See? I am not different. You have nothing to fear. I am as safe as you." And he may be. But what about the millions of people who will never have the refuge of the good life, who cannot be honest because their very lives would be in danger. Homosexuality is not simply a social handicap; nor is it the exclusive property of lonely little boys growing up in small, insensitive towns in the Midwest. To American morality, it is a perversion and is treated accordingly. It is also a rich, rewarding experience for many, a sort of model for totally free people if they can break through to the other side.

But Mr. Miller doesn't want to make any total break-through. He didn't like suffering because he was different, and so he thinks homosexuality should be recognized as not being different. *But there is nothing wrong with being different.* Although he is against anyone's being condemned because he is a homosexual, he still subscribes to the attitudes that make such cruelty possible. He was a "sissy" as a child; he worked hard to overcome that stigma, but it kept reappearing, evidently, through a failed marriage and unpleasant encounters with people who questioned his masculinity. Finally he got it all off his chest. But his admission consisted of realizing that he was unacceptable in the eyes of society and hoping the society could still accommodate him, accepting him back into its good graces. I had hoped, somewhere in the back of my mind, that he would tell society to go fuck itself, that he could be effeminate or masculine or any damn thing he wanted to.

I was disappointed in the article. I didn't see how it could really offend people or make them question any of their comfortably straight biases. But I was wrong. The article upset many people. The most vocal was Andrew Sarris, the widely read and respected film critic of the *Village Voice*.

Sarris left his usual province to do an extraordinary two-part attack on Miller's article and the gay liberation movement in general. What seems to have offended Sarris most is not what Miller said but that he said anything at all. The gist of Sarris's diatribe seemed to be that he had enough problems without having to worry about some dizzy faggot. He talks about "accumulating guilt at an alarming rate" over the Jews, the blacks, the American Indians, as well as Hiroshima, Biafra, Haiti, Pakistan, and so on, until finally he has reached a point where he must draw the line and go no further. His furious attack on homosexuals is much more revealing and probably even more helpful for homosexuals than Miller's somewhat self-centered piece.

Sarris says, near the beginning of his article, "The fact remains, however, that heteros have never had it all that easy as a class in Puritanical America where until very recently a male whore was easier to pick up than a female whore, and a buddy made a less scandalous roommate than a girl friend." Oh yeah? Reading this unnerved me—perhaps it was as if I were a black reading about the difficulty of getting good help today. Later, Sarris says that the "aggressive homosexual does not ask for pity or kindness. He prefers to ridicule many of the myths and feelings I revere." God forbid that a homosexual would not need Andrew Sarris's approval, that he might even *dislike* what Sarris stands for. Finally, as his clincher, Sarris throws out the standard technique used by sophisticated heterosexuals to placate and shut up homosexuals. "Every homosexual, like every heterosexual, is something more and something other than his sexual personality. And that is where this male heterosexual takes his stand: with the something more, the something other, the something extra that redeems the relative banality and poverty of sexual 'techniques' in human existence. Wilde, Proust, Auden, Forster are not so much homosexuals who happened to be great artists as great artists who happened to be homosexuals." In other words, it's all just a matter of the breaks.

What never occurs to Sarris is that these men are homosexuals *and* artists. Their homosexuality does not have to be subordinated to anything, least of all to spare the sensibilities of anyone like Sarris. There were several other points of criticism in Sarris's article, lambasting Miller and other writers for equally ill-defined crimes, including the use of their "confessional gush" as part of a phony new industry of interpersonal technology; he also implies that their "illusory" attempts at telling the truth are self-serving attempts at some sort of personal gains—perhaps more people to go to bed with?

It disturbed me that a critical article by a straight man would awaken a much stronger response in me than an article by a gay man trying to express solidarity with me. But Miller's piece was so full of admitted self-hate and of contempt for the "effeminate" type despised by straight society that I could not really see very much that was new, nor could I empathize with him personally. Sarris, on the other hand, is a classically hostile straight male; the fags are out to get him and ruin his world, and he fights back with all he's got. I was a little disappointed to see that his second installment, published a week later, had regained most of the composure standard in such a liberal mind. Now, we were all in this together; he doesn't care what people do personally; let's just each go about trying to make the world a little better. These softening remarks make Sarris appear not only bigoted but stupid. It is better to keep it all up front; he doesn't like homosexuals, is insulted if anyone implies that he could be a homosexual, and wants homosexuals to keep their business to themselves. He is the embodiment of the straight, hip man.

One of the confessional gushers Sarris blithely disparaged is Jill Johnston, another writer for the *Voice* who has turned her column on dance into a fascinating, sometimes boring, infuriating, funny account of one woman's radicalization into a lesbian. Because she is thought to be avant-garde and she is, after all, a woman, and a women's liberation freak at that, her assertions of her homosexuality are not taken as seriously by Sarris and others as was Miller's innocuous little piece. But, when she replied to Sarris in her column, she said, "I'm going on record here to notify every heterosexual male and female that every lesbian and every homosexual is all too aware of the problems of heterosexuals since they permeate every aspect of our social political economic and cultural lives. That we were in fact educated on these problems. That we were brought up and spoon fed or pitch forked on the crucible of the problems of thousands of Romeos and Juliets radiating outward from all our sublimely miserable and broken families into the movies and the funnies and the histories and the psychologies and the novels and our great Western classics." That seems to me to be an ultimate comment on the unsuitability of homosexuals daring to discuss themselves in the media.

The *Village Voice,* incidentally, has evidently finally decided to give homosexuals equal time, after its long history of deriding them. A series of clumsy but sincere articles by Arthur Bell was recently followed by several pieces from Stuart Byron, a film critic, who declared that he would be a hypocrite if he didn't express his interest in a good-looking man's performance in a film, just the way Sarris occasionally drools over women in *his* reviews. Much more significantly, Byron provided an incisive account of how and why the *New York Times* has consistently attempted to bury all coverage of positive news concerning homosexuals, while playing up the homosexuals-are-sick-but-might-be-cured school. Byron judiciously avoids asking the obvious question that I, a plain old biased reader, automatically ask: what does the *Times* have to gain by keeping homosexuals down?

These may seem like parochial squabbles, of little meaning in a homosexual's real life. But I think they are important issues; homosexuals have a right to see their community as it exists, every side of it. Homosexuals are no more homogeneous than any other minority group; the fact that they are not even supposed to exist in the eyes of the straight world makes the possibility of comprehensive, fair-minded coverage very remote. It seems necessary for the radicalization of an individual and the growth of his personal freedom that he first find out what is really going on in his world. It is important that younger homosexuals find out that, while they are hitting six bars a night, looking for a good lay, there are people working on laws about bias in employment practices. It is important that radical homosexuals who are seeking to organize a new revolutionary force realize that there are thirty-year-old suburban fathers who have had sex with scores of men and never said a single word to any of them. It is important that older homosexuals who have spent decades trying to pass as straight see that there are young women and men who revel in their sexuality and literally shout their gayness to the whole world. There will be no widespread homosexual revolution until these older men and their female counterparts are reached. If it takes the *New York Times* and other bourgeois institutions to do it, then they should be confronted and changed as soon as possible. Ideally a small-town weekly should be just as free to print an announcement of a homosexual meeting or dance as it is to run notices about church thrift sales and PTA meetings.

Visual media are potentially even more powerful for re-educating people about homosexuality. Unfortunately, their impact thus far has been negligible. Television has produced very little to counter the years of jokes about fairies, queens, and limp wrists that have been spouted at us by Bob Hope, Carol Burnett, Johnny Carson, and even Dick Cavett, the new nighttime "intellectual." Cavett, however, did set a precedent when he had two members of the Gay Activists' Alliance and the former president of the New York Mattachine Society on his show. Despite Cavett's puzzled and wary reluctance to accept the possibility of any reforms other than an end to obvious police harassment and greater job security, the show was a milestone. It was the first occasion where the oppression of homosexuals was discussed on TV with intelligence and at length.

There was an appearance by two lesbians on the "Today" show, which I missed but which I hope disturbed Middle America's breakfast. There was a standard melodrama on the TV series "Medical Center," wherein a young doctor's career was threatened by anonymous, evidently obscene notes denouncing him as a homosexual. The twist here was that, after a great flap about one's right to be considered innocent until proven guilty, the cowardice of poison-pen letter-writers, and so on, the young doctor suddenly admitted that he was homosexual—unhappy about it, but determinedly homosexual. I made a point of watching that show, although I have tried to miss most network programs for years. I hoped for some sort of notice afterwards, either approving or distraught, anything to prove to people that there really were doctors—and maybe even, lawyers, priests, students, *children*—who were gay. I didn't detect any reaction in the press, which is perhaps just as well. I would not like to see homosexuality exploited at the level where black-white conflicts, abortion, and euthanasia are—to sell soap and dog food.

Very recently, David Susskind presented four male gay activists on his talk show. But, because he evidently felt that the public was unprepared for the shock of seeing four men who were happy homosexuals—as these men were, despite their diverse backgrounds and philosophies—Susskind also presented four "cured" homosexuals. This latter group, monopolizing the conversation, discussed their cure, which was caused by some crackpot philosophy called Aesthetic

Realism. Once again, the gay audience was deeply disappointed. There are several million gay people in this country; there are one hundred and fifty Aesthetic Realists. Yet gay life was so frightening to Susskind that he could not simply let four homosexuals appear and state their case; the straight world had to be sure that homosexuality was kept in its proper perspective—that is, as a sickness.

Movies are now the frankest portrayers of homosexuality, and the most disappointing. In an era when virtually anything short of hard-core fucking can be shown in a first-run theater, the legitimate problems of homosexuals are denied the attention given to the problems of unwed mothers, lecherous writers, gangsters, airline stewardesses, housewives, and countless others (all of whom can often be homosexuals in real life). The enormously complicated relationship between homosexuality and films is a topic that deserves a long book of its own; here I will attempt to discuss my own personal reactions to homosexuality on the screen.

Movies have been the source of our myths in this century. Tens of millions of American children have grown up on movies and stars. It is no accident that John Wayne and Vietnam are inextricable. The continuing fascination for James Dean and Marilyn Monroe are not so much macabre oddities as a fierce national attachment to some sort of squandered innocence. It is not only *Easy Rider* and *Wild Angels* that have helped shape a life style for today's young; there are also vast young audiences for films as dissimilar as *Love Story*, *M.A.S.H.*, and *Five Easy Pieces*. Even though today's young people are much more sophisticated than their parents were at the same age, they derive pleasure and even inspiration from all kinds of films, as did their parents. The best films that they enjoy have kept pace and are now much more frank than anything a filmgoer of the forties could have imagined.

Except in one area. Homosexuality has always been taboo

on the screen, unless it was disguised in some sort of comedy routine—fairy salesman waits on hero customer, prissy butler is frightened by hero's girlfriend, and so on. There were a few very subtle, carefully disguised attempts to show real homosexuality—Robert Walker's nervously polite psychopath in Hitchcock's *Strangers on a Train* or the fadeout in *All About Eve*, when the cynical, successful actress wearily invites a strange young girl to stay with her. Even in these cases, homosexuality was equated with sick, even deranged personalities. The depiction of homosexuals as *relatively* normal people is a recent development, starting with the extremely belated film version of Lillian Hellmann's *The Children's Hour*. The only earlier example I can think of is *Tea and Sympathy*, which I saw as a teen-ager. I remember the heroine, a married woman, finally putting her foot down and refusing to condemn a young student for various unspeakable perversions—evidently homosexual. She saves the student from the possibility of a vicious beating and from the curse of homosexuality—by seducing him.

It is interesting to note that the depiction of homosexual relationships between women were portrayed vividly long before the existence of active male homosexuality was even implied. In *The Children's Hour*, two women teachers are accused of having homosexual relations. When it develops that one of the women does actually have homosexual feelings, she hangs herself. In the later adaptation of D. H. Lawrence's *The Fox*, two lesbians give shelter to a young man, who decides to fall in love with one of the women. A huge tree conveniently falls on the other, thus enabling the man to take his "rightful" place. *The Killing of Sister George* —which was written by a man and was previously a great stage success—presents a cynical, downbeat picture of two lesbians who are casually wrecking each other's lives when a third woman steps in to break up their household for good. Despite excellent performances by actresses who succeed in injecting a little realism to it, the film seems to serve no other function than to provide audiences with the spectacle of three freaks who at least lead more miserable lives than the viewers.

There have been endless variations on the lesbian-as-sick-woman theme, from the frustrated and eventually psychotic schoolteacher in *Night of the Iguana* to the fierce misanthrope in *Five Easy Pieces* who has a fixation about polluting the environment. The only films that do not show lesbians as sick show them as sex objects. An example is Radley Metzger's ludicrous *Therese and Isabelle*, which was adapted from a fine book by a French lesbian, Violette LeDuc. The displaying of lesbians as sexual stimuli for straight males has frightening implications; it is the worst kind of exploitation of women, a gross distortion of the way a whole group of people lives.

Men have fared no better. To my knowledge, the first reference to active homosexuality in films was Elizabeth Taylor's harrowing recital, in *Suddenly Last Summer*, of her cousin's seduction of poor Spanish boys and their eventual revenge on him—cannibalism. The Tennessee Williams vision of homosexuality has dominated the stage and to a lesser extent the screen since the topic was able to be discussed at all; his view of the homosexual as some sort of fallen angel who must perish because he is a misfit may have some viability within his own work, but it is also comforting to the straight world, which is reinforced in its revulsion at homosexuality. *Suddenly Last Summer* was the ultimate example: fuck around with boys and you will be destroyed. The wages of sin, in a nutshell. It stands in contrast to roughly contemporary (early 1950's) *Tea and Sympathy*, where the hero earns the "right" to live by renouncing homosexuality.

Foreign films explored homosexuality in their own way (*The Leather Boys* from England, *The Damned* from Italy), with more taste, but equally unhappy results. Homosexuals were rejected or killed or used as symbols of ultimate depravity. It was left to America to produce the first "real" homosexual film, *The Boys in the Band*. I have had hours of discussions with friends over this film. To many, it is the most visible result of a new homosexual mentality; that a film about male homosexuals who actually *are* homosexuals could be widely distributed is amazing. Yet isn't it possible that the widespread success of the film shows only that there is a market for films that portray homosexuals in situations corresponding roughly with reality, dealing with the trivia that most people worry about, with little possibility of a violent death waiting round the corner to punish them?

My objections to this film are extremely basic, and yet perhaps oversubtle. I have never been to a party like the one shown in the film, nor have I ever seen a group of people play a self-destructive "game" with such avidity. I have encountered homosexuals who lived like the people in the film. No one has claimed any great artistic merit for the film, but many people (ranging from stanch Republicans to weary, older radicals) think that the film does accurately portray a certain kind of life. I agree, but I would add that the portrait is of only one segment of the homosexual population. The self-pity, the hatred for the freak in oneself, the scorn for the man who dares to act like a woman—all of these reflect straight society's scorn for homosexuals, which homosexuals incorporate by association. There are men in this film who seem to be functioning fairly well; a few even seem to come a little closer to resolving such mundane but very real problems as infidelity, the need for material acquisitions, the inability to see oneself as anything but a caricature. But, when the crises inevitably come, they accept themselves as somehow unhappy *because* they are homosexuals and see very little prospect for anything except learning to bear the burden manfully.

This is simply not true; life is never as vividly black and

white as it is on the screen, and it is certainly never as despairingly simple as *The Boys in the Band* pictures it. Homosexuals are faced with a number of options besides despair and stoic resignation. *The Boys in the Band* is, in essence, a political film; it describes a class and infers generalizations from what it shows. To me, it is thus a failure; the generalizations and inferences it draws are false, because they come out of the false consciousness of straight society, rather than the humanity of its protagonists. I certainly can't determine what was in the mind of the writer, Mart Crowley; I only know that his work simply confirms all the biases that straight people—and homosexuals—have held for centuries about homosexuals. It is interesting to note that, in the course of the film, no man ever kissed another, although there were several references to physical sex; evidently, there are still things that cannot be shown, except in pornography.

A few years ago, Donn Teal wrote an article in the *New York Times* asking why there could be no plays or films about homosexuals with happy endings. Jill Johnston recently made the same suggestion, somewhat reluctantly, as an antidote to the incredible lack of realism about homosexuality that the media have perpetuated. I can't quite agree. I don't think homosexuals deserve or need "happy" endings any more than anyone else. But they do deserve to be told the truth, after all these years, and they do deserve to be allowed to make up their own minds. Being a homosexual does not mean that you should have to suffer any more than the rest of mankind, and all the films and plays and novels and poems that say you do are either descriptions of outdated attitudes or lies. I have known homosexuals who were psychologically and spiritually among the strongest people I have ever encountered; they had to be, to survive. They were not destructive, of themselves or others. And they were not isolated examples or freaks; their one common characteristic was that they realized that it was dangerous to be gay. But we (humanity) have hopefully come far enough that we can recognize those fears as constricting and pointless, and move out beyond them. I want to see their lives portrayed; I want to see, on a screen or on a stage, homosexuals whose solutions to their lives consist of more than breaking down under the opprobrium of the straight world or suffering in silence. There *is* a new homosexual consciousness emerging, and it should be seen as soon as possible in all the media.

• • •

All the changes, and potential changes, listed above are important. But, in my experience, the greatest and most direct changes are those wrought in concrete circumstances, in people's own lives and daily encounters. And that is where homosexual liberation finds its ultimate test and proves itself.

I have already mentioned how I suddenly found myself dropping out. Without intending to do so, I had completely altered the way I live. It is extraordinary how many times I have seen this happen among people who are involved in gay liberation. It seems to be such a sensible process when you are living through it, but it evidently doesn't make any sense at all to those who don't, as the numerous bewildered queries of old friends show. When people ask me what exactly am I trying to do, I find it very hard to produce a specific answer. But that certainly does not mean that I am not trying to do something.

When you become totally dissatisfied with a way of living, you look for another way (unless you are lazy or a fool). I was dissatisfied with pretending to be straight. I was dissatisfied with pretending to enjoy the struggle to get ahead in the publishing world. I was discontented being a closet homosexual, hiding the most important parts of my life from everyone except myself, savoring them like some old miser.

So I stopped doing what I didn't want to do, and started trying to do something new.

And that is perhaps an analogy for the dilemma and for the promise of the whole gay liberation movement. Radical homosexuals certainly don't want to be straight—some homosexuals do, but they are by definition certainly not radical homosexuals; their decision is only another painful example of the heterosexual intimidation of the homosexual. Radical homosexuals don't want to relate to gay life as they did before. So we are literally up front: we can't go back, and we can't go sideways. Out of an urgent practical necessity, we have to be a new kind of people. This is not simply a matter of dropping out into the Woodstock nation; there is enough fear and distrust of homosexuality among hip and radical straight people to make us realize that the Woodstock nation stands a very good chance of being nothing more than an updated, dope-filled spinoff of the straight consumer society.

I have not yet been convinced that large groups offer opportunities for massive changes among homosexuals. My experiences in small groups have been the most decisive in my personal development; the consciousness-raising groups described earlier have fulfilled their potential more fully than any other activity coming out of gay liberation. It is difficult to convey the subtle changes and realizations that can be reached in these groups; part of the problem in communicating them is perhaps due to the technical-sounding name and the seemingly rigid format. I would encourage anyone who is interested in getting into a group to do so. These groups are not nearly as grim as they might sound.

After the first group I was in drifted apart, I took stock and realized that we had accomplished a great deal. We may have lost contact with each other earlier than some of us wanted to, but that was because of external factors—jobs, going back to school, financial strains. But we also were still very unsure of what we were trying to do. So, when I decided that I would like to get into another group, I tried to figure out what would make this group work better than the last one. It turned out that the group did indeed work better, but not as I had planned; it seems that planning anything just doesn't work anymore.

I contacted several people I was already acquainted with, none of whom had been in a group. Only a few were interested, and, after we started meeting, three of them dropped out. We were left with a core of seven, the number as of this writing; that may be too few, and we are trying to interest a few more people in joining us. But, in the five months or so that we have been getting together, I have seen changes take place in other members' lives that have been at least as radical as anything I have undergone. These changes occur not so much in our day-to-day routines; for example, most of the group went fairly regularly to gay bars and still go. But there is an increasing boredom with the unwritten code that governs behavior there: be cool; don't talk to people who aren't cool; go to the places where the hippest people go; don't go home with anyone unless he's something special. The men in the group quickly came to see that, unless you are going to a gay bar just to drink—often a very expensive deal—you had better realize that it is pretty unlikely you will meet the most beautiful boy in the world. A gay bar was once a convenient place when homosexuals could not openly express themselves in other places, but now it is an anachronism. I was never very interested in going to gay bars; I always felt threatened by the need to be even more on guard than usual. But, curiously enough, now I am beginning to loosen up, to appreciate the fact that these bars were for many years the only communal places homosexuals had.

The more basic changes involve attitudes about things that generally are not considered to involve homosexuality. Three of the people in our group are teachers. Independently, they have all raised the question about their dual functions as homosexuals and teachers. One teaches college-age art students; one counsels college students with "problem" backgrounds; one teaches preschool children at an expensive, progressive private school. All have realized that they are programing students to live in a heterosexual world. Just as the possibility of homosexuality was left for them to discover by themselves, so their students are being sheltered from contact with an important part of their teachers' lives. These men are beginning to question the compatibility of living as a supposedly well-adjusted homosexual while denying in their work the existence of homosexuality.

One of the men in our group is black. He recently raised the question of racism among homosexuals; the rest of us were reluctant to discuss it. We had all heard the arguments accusing us of being racists before, and, like good liberals, we acquiesced, said it was inevitable, and were ready to move on. But he insisted on exploring the topic, and got angry when we were lethargic. And it worked. It was not a pleasant or gratifying experience, and none of us came away with the good feelings that a cursory confession of racism is intended to produce. We weren't talking about sitting next to black people in school or helping them get voting rights or discussing the possible result of black militance. We were talking about fucking with black men, and that brings out the most basic attitudes and generalizations in a person. Were we hostile to or frightened of blacks in sexual encounters? If so, why? The answers were very slow and painful in coming, but they were far more true than most of what I had ever before felt about race.

Some of our most violent and long-winded discussions revolved around the question of love and intimate relationships. I do not intend to discuss the possibility of love in homosexuality, which needs no more, or no less, analysis than the possibility of love among heterosexuals. Because we felt no need to justify ourselves as homosexuals, we naturally considered the possibility of deeply loving, sexually, another man. To heterosexuals, the concept of love among homosexuals remains a mystery and something of a joke, but homosexuals share in the same desires for warmth and responsiveness, the same need for someone to communicate with. Homosexuals worry about being loved just as do heterosexuals. Moreover, they are raised with the same myths, the same Hollywood-advertising-Judaeo-Christian-marriage complex that still governs most relationships in this country. Homosexuals, perhaps even more than straight people, have been forced into looking for the "right" one, someone who will give their lives some meaning and shape. And that search has usually ended in failure and apathy or bitterness, just as it has for heterosexuals.

We all considered ourselves intelligent. Not only did we all have bachelor's degrees, but we had all done graduate work as well. So it was embarrassing when the old, corny words kept coming up—"love," "looking for somebody," "fulfillment," "need." But these were part of our deepest expectations, and we hadn't become so hip that we could discard them. Gradually, in our discussions, we realized that each of us was coming to a new sort of recognition about what we wanted out of relationships, based on our experiences as homosexuals. The traditional promiscuity of homosexuality, the numerous affairs and lovers that an "average" homosexual supposedly experiences, all have a positive value. Once you realize that the standard values of a lifelong monogamous marriage are not necessary to a new kind of American culture or to your life and may, in fact, even be destructive, it is easy to see that having experiences with many people may strengthen you, rather than be a symptom of moral decay. It is certainly possible that any of us in the group might meet someone whom he responds to—whom he really "loves"—and spend the rest of his life with that person.

It is also possible that he may live his life alone, while having encounters that can mean a great deal to him. There is no ideal. The only things to avoid are the limits that one forces on oneself—the need for someone else to complete your life, the need for someone else to take care of you, the compulsion to be on top, physically and psychologically.

Our group helped me and others to continue to realize what we could be. I found out again, more deeply, that I could do whatever I wanted. It was strangely like the old Protestant ethic—anything is possible, if you're willing to work hard enough for it.

· · ·

To close this book, I would like to make a series of proposals that involve gay liberation. These are not put forth as any sweeping proclamations; rather, they are suggestions for a more realistic and workable approach to homosexuality and gay life. They are *not* presented for the approval of straight people; they are aimed at homosexuals, as observations about gay life. I expect some heterosexuals will be outraged, but that should not affect the possibility that gay people will work with these ideas. Straight people have been outraged for centuries about gay life, and they have been wrong all along. It's time for them to start changing, too.

● Education must be revised to include the depiction of homosexuality and lesbianism as life styles that exist, rather than as unacknowledged secrets. It seems sensible to begin this as soon as possible, preferably in conjunction with present sex education programs. Shocking at first (even to many homosexuals, including myself), this proposal should not be feared as indoctrination; it is no more dangerous than the heterosexual propaganda that has jammed children into increasingly irrelevant roles. Homosexual teachers should not be barred from teaching any age group. Here, I suppose, is the place to state that homosexuals are no more likely to molest children than are heterosexuals; a man who is attracted to small children may be a homosexual, but his sickness is not homosexuality, just as man who molests little girls does not have the sickness of heterosexuality.

● Antihomosexual jokes, comedy routines, and caricatures should be immediately eliminated from the media, and there should be no more of the slanderous "hip" rhetoric that labels those whom one is supposed to hate—Nixon, Mitchell, *et al.*—as faggots, cocksuckers, fairies. Certainly, reasoned public discussions for and against homosexuality should take place, but to continue to deride gay people is as offensive as continuing to call women chicks or broads, to call Jews kikes, to call blacks niggers. The self-hatred that psychiatrists pounce on as characteristic of all gay life is only the internalization of this contemptuous abuse and will fade away when the abuse does.

● All laws forbidding homosexual activities between individuals of any age should be abolished. Specifications about "consenting adults" and "in private" are unnecessary and unenforceable. Teen-age couples have been making out and having sex in parked cars since there were parked cars; they have not been legislated against. Homosexuals do not try to embarrass straight people by overt sexual activity; rather, our society is embarrassed by overt sexual activity of any kind.

● Homosexual and multisexual households of two or more individuals should be recognized and given all the tax benefits, insurance provisions, social services, and community resources that traditional families receive and use. There should also be an equalization of such matters for people who live alone; they are unfairly saddled with supporting services for a family-oriented society that is heading for overpopulation.

● Homosexuals' drive for their rights should be recognized

by other reformist and revolutionary groups. Women's liberation groups were the first, and have been thus far the most enthusiastic, supporters of gay liberation, perhaps because they see that lesbians are, at once, the most oppressed and the most free women. Hopefully, third-world people will also recognize that their self-expression is inextricably bound up with the aims of gay liberation, which revolve primarily around the destruction of the white male-supremacist oligarchy that controls the United States and the rest of the world.

● Homosexuals should openly acknowledge their homosexuality wherever possible—at jobs, in universities and high schools, with parents and other relatives, among holders of public office, in the media and the arts, even in the military. This should not be interpreted as an encouragement of confessions, but rather an affirmation of what it means to be homosexual. Many homosexuals cannot, for a variety of reasons, speak out openly yet about their homosexuality; thus, it becomes even more urgent that those who can do.

● Small groups should be formed in which homosexuals can discuss in depth their experiences, their oppression, and possible changes in life style. These informal, intimate, supportive groups would give gay liberation a concrete meaning in the lives of individual homosexuals. Meanwhile, homosexuals could, according to their political persuasion, support the aims of larger groups, such as the Gay Liberation Front, the Daughters of Bilitis, the Gay Activists' Alliance, and the Mattachine Society, and work with them, publicly or behind the scenes.

● New centers for gay life should be created—community centers, coffeehouses, perhaps even bars, which, in addition to being places where one can meet a partner, would serve as clearing houses for information and would provide space for community activities and sources of help and orientation for young people. These should be established in commu-

nities of all sizes and not be confined merely to large cities.
● It should be stressed continually that gay liberation is not
simply a one-issue reform movement. The forces that have
oppressed homosexuals for so long are the same ones that
have allowed and encouraged racism, contempt for women,
and belief in war as the ultimate test of masculine strength.
We cannot deal with homosexuality in our society today
unless we realize that our problems are enormously aggra-
vated by a system of values in which advertising sets ultimate
standards, sex and love are in danger of becoming marketable
commodities, and money, sex, and power have become virtually identical. We cannot merely change some piece of our
world that encompasses homosexuality. We have to change
the whole, or we will accomplish nothing.

The above suggestions could perhaps be extended indefi-
nitely. I repeat that they are the thoughts of one person
speaking from his own experiences. If any other lesbian or
homosexual were questioned, an entirely different list might
result. And that would be good: we should all have these
lists. When we begin to put them together and continue what
we have started, we will not be stopped.

This book belongs to

**THE GAY ALLIANCE
OF
PRINCETON**

306 Aaron Burr Hall
Princeton University
Princeton, N.J. 08544
(609) 452-5338